"ONE SHOT"

THE WORLD WAR II PHOTOGRAPHY OF

JOHN A. BUSHEMI

ON LEAVE FROM THE ARMY, JOHN BUSHEMI POSES WITH
HIS SISTER MARY ELLEN NEAR THEIR HOME IN GARY.

Best wishes,

Ray Th

ENTER THE SHOT

THE WORLD WAR II PHOTOGRAPHY OF
JOHN A. BUSHEMI

INTRODUCTION BY

INDIANA HISTORICAL SOCIETY PRESS

Printed in China

This book is a publication of the
Indiana Historical Society Press
450 West Ohio Street
Indianapolis, Indiana 46202-3269 USA
www.indianahistory.org
Telephone orders 1-800-447-1830
Fax orders 317-234-0562
Orders by E-mail shop.indianahistory.org

The paper in this publication meets the minimum requirements of American National Standard for Information Sciences—Permanence of Paper for Printed Library Materials, ANSI Z39.48-1984

Library of Congress Cataloging-Publication Data

Boomhower, Ray E., 1959-
  One shot : the World War II photography of John A. Bushemi / Ray E. Boomhower : introduction by James H. Madison.
    p.   cm.
  Includes bibliographical references.
  ISBN 0-87195-174-6 (cloth : alk. paper)
    1. Bushemi, John. 2. World War, 1939-1945—Photography. 3. World War, 1939-1945—Pictorial works. 4. War photographers—United States—Biography. I. Title.

D810.P4B66 2004
940.54'1273'092—dc22
[B]
                                                    2003069167

Portions of this book previously appeared in the winter 2002 issue of *Traces of Indiana and Midwestern History.*

THIS BOOK IS DEDICATED TO THE MEMORY
OF MY FATHER-IN-LAW, DR. ROY MCKEE,
AN AIR FORCE PHYSICIAN DURING THE
KOREAN WAR. YEARS EARLIER A DEAR
FRIEND OF HIS FROM KANSAS CITY DIED
DURING THE INVASION OF TARAWA.
ROY WAS A LOVING HUSBAND AND A
DEVOTED FATHER AND IS DEEPLY MISSED.

CONTENTS

PREFACE

On April 7, 2001, members of the Indiana Journalism Hall of Fame board of directors gathered together with colleagues, friends, and family members to honor four new inductees into the organization's Hall of Fame in ceremonies at the Walden Inn on the campus of DePauw University in Greencastle, Indiana. As one of the board members for the association, I mingled with the other guests before the induction luncheon. In reviewing the program for the day's event, I realized that I knew quite a bit about three of the four inductees. Of particular interest to me was Juliet V. Strauss, a former columnist for the *Rockville Tribune*, *Indianapolis News*, and *Ladies' Home Journal*, whose career I had chronicled in an article for the Indiana Historical Society's popular history magazine *Traces of Indiana and Midwestern History* and in a biography for Guild Press of Indiana. I happily greeted her great-great-grandchildren, Cynthia and Andrew Snowden, who had provided assistance to me in producing the work on Strauss.

After welcoming the Snowdens, I congratulated inductee G. Patrick Siddons, who had served as publisher and adviser to the *Indiana Daily Student* at Indiana University during my own days as a writer and editor for the student newspaper. As the crowd sat down for lunch, I met Dean Reynolds, who was at the ceremonies to accept the honor for his late father, ABC television newsman and anchor Frank Reynolds. As the luncheon proceeded, I noticed a large group of people gathered at another table. I later learned that these were relatives of the fourth inductee, John A. Bushemi, former photographer for the *Gary Post-Tribune* who had been killed in combat in the Pacific during World War II while on assignment for the GI magazine *Yank*. As Bushemi's nephew, John P. Bushemi, a Merrillville attorney, talked about his late uncle's accomplishments, I became more and more impressed by the photographer's life and resolved to look into his career.

As someone who has always been interested in the history of World War II, I quickly became intrigued with Bushemi and his work in the Pacific theater on such far-flung operations as New Georgia, Makin, Tarawa, Kwajalein, and Eniwetok. My research on Bushemi's career also introduced me to the fascinating story of *Yank*, a periodical devoted to producing a view of the war for the average enlisted man. My interest in Bushemi resulted in an article for *Traces*, for which I serve as managing editor. My piece appeared in the winter 2002 issue as "John A. Bushemi: Combat Photographer." To me, however, there seemed to be much more to say about Bushemi's life than could fit in the confines of a magazine article. I continued to find—with the help of Bushemi family members and former *Yank* associates—information on the photographer's career. The result of all this labor is the book you now hold in your hands.

Writing is often portrayed as a lonely business with ink-stained wretches struggling over their typewriters (or computers) to produce their work. The process of writing a biography, however, often entails a more cooperative spirit. Conducting research means that a biographer needs to deal with a variety of individuals—archivists, librarians, friends, family, and others associated with the subject being written about.

Ronnie Day, professor of history and chair of the history department at East Tennessee State University, provided invaluable assistance on Bushemi's career at *Yank* magazine, particularly the photographer's partnership with correspondent Mack Morriss. Dr. Day's encouragement and assistance on this project gives true meaning to the term scholar.

Another noted writer and historian, James H. Madison, professor of history at Indiana University, graciously agreed to provide an essay on Indiana and World War II to provide context for Bushemi's life and career. It's an honor to be in the same publication with a historian of Dr. Madison's stature.

My thanks to Bushemi's *Yank* colleague Marion Hargrove, who shared recollections of his friend "Bush" during a telephone interview from his home in Santa Monica, California. I am pleased to bring to readers the story of the friendship between the photographer from the Calumet Region and the writer from North Carolina. Unfortunately, the eighty-three-year-old Hargrove did not live to see the book in production. He passed away on August 23, 2003, in a Long Beach, California, hospice due to complications from pneumonia.

I also offer my appreciation to the staffs at the Prints and Photographs Division at the Library of Congress, the U.S. Military History Institute at Carlisle Barracks, the DePauw University Archives and Special Collections, and Indiana University Library in Bloomington for their help in securing the documents, photographs, and other materials needed for researching and publishing this book. Jane Rustin, director of the Wayne County Public Library in Goldsboro, North Carolina, and Gary Barefoot of the Friends of the Steele Memorial Library Branch in Mount Olive, North Carolina, were of particular help in obtaining information on Hargrove's career. My thanks also to Stephen McShane, archivist/curator of the Calumet Regional Archives at Indiana University Northwest in Gary, Indiana. Two Indiana Historical Society William Henry Smith Memorial Library staff members—Susan Sutton, coordinator, visual reference services, and Kim Charles Ferrill, former photographer—were of great help in reproducing photographs for the book.

As usual, the editors at the Indiana Historical Society Press—Paula Corpuz, Doug Clanin, Kathy Breen, George Hanlin, and Judith McMullen—offered encouragement when needed and correction when necessary when dealing with the manuscript. My wife, Megan McKee, as she has done on my four other books, used her keen editorial skills to help sharpen my writing. Of course, any mistakes in the book are mine and mine alone.

This work truly would not have been possible without the guidance and encouragement of Bushemi's sister, Mary Ellen Cessna, and her son, Kevin Cessna. Both Mary Ellen and Kevin sat and talked with me for hours about their famous relative and made available to me scrapbooks, photographs, and other material about his life. I hope they are pleased with the results of my efforts.

JAPANESE
SURRENDER
5TH EXTRA
JAPANESE
SURRENDER
THE INDIANAPOLIS NEWS
JAPANESE
SURRENDER
5TH EXTRA

HOME FRONT, BATTLEFRONT, AND THE "GOOD WAR"

JAMES H. MADISON

World War II was a total war, so massive and complex that no one person could see through the fog—not during the years 1941–45 and still not today. John A. Bushemi was one among millions who attempted to understand the war and one of many thousands whose job it was to explain its meaning to other Americans. His work and that of other photographers, filmmakers, reporters, and propagandists was essential to victory because understanding the war was prerequisite to the large sacrifices this war demanded. Americans in uniform and civilians on the home front needed to know that the necessities of war and of victory required them to make such sacrifices. They needed to understand why.

There were consequences to the way Americans came to understand World War II. Many gained particularly upbeat notions about the war and its place in the larger sweep of world history, notions that decades later would incorporate such labels as the "good war" and the "greatest generation ever." They came to believe that this war represented the best of American ideals; that it was about the American way of life so directly threatened by the Axis powers; that it was evidence of America's inevitable triumph over evil. As time passed many forgot the brutalities of the war, the ambiguities and complexities, the doubts and mistakes. They moved to a simpler, cleaner memory—one that tended to picture the past in terms of good and bad and right and wrong, with the shades of gray deleted from memory.[1]

December 7, 1941, not only left much of the Pacific fleet at the bottom of the Pearl Harbor but also let loose a string of quick Japanese victories in Asia and across the Pacific. The German swastika already flew over most of the European continent. In the dark months of early 1942, Americans prepared for the worst. Where would the enemy attack next? Indiana's General Assembly created a State Defense council in 1941 on the assumption that the Hoosier State was "a logical target for attack." Blackout drills became the order of the day.[2]

But the most important challenge facing Americans at home was not the threat of Axis bombs. The real challenge was to mobilize the economy. America had to become the "great arsenal of democracy," as President Franklin D.

Roosevelt urged, because this very modern war would be won only with massive factory production as well as foxhole heroism. Indiana factories converted to producing war goods, transitioning from autos to tanks, from refrigerators to bomb cases. Among Indiana's largest contributions was aircraft production, led by Allison Division of General Motors in Indianapolis, which manufactured engines for pursuit planes. Others included Curtiss-Wright also in Indianapolis, Republic Aviation in Evansville, and Bendix in South Bend. Trucks poured off the lines at International Harvester in Fort Wayne and Studebaker in South Bend. New production sprang to life at the shipyards in Evansville and Jeffersonville and at the Charlestown and Kingsbury munitions plants. The Calumet Region's steel and petroleum output rose to new levels. Indianapolis's Eli Lilly and Company shipped tons of blood plasma and penicillin. When the totals were calculated at war's end, Indiana ranked third in the nation in per capita war production.[3]

Factories needed workers. With growing numbers of healthy young men going off to war, employers sought new labor pools. Women were the most obvious choice. One of the most important necessities of this war was the employment of women in jobs that had heretofore been thought appropriate only for men. With their hair cut short

or tied in a bandana, their bodies obscured in work clothes, their nails broken and dirty, women did their part. Employers began active recruitment of women to their factories in late 1942. A year later, women made up more than a third of Indiana's factory workers. They faced many challenges. Often their pay was lower than that of men doing the same job; unions sometimes treated them as second-class workers; child care for working mothers was limited, if available at all; and male co-workers sometimes welcomed them and sometimes gave them the cold shoulder or more active harassment, in part because some men were confused by this assault on traditional definitions of women's roles. In the end, it's hard to imagine defeat of the Axis without the contributions of American working women in factories, farms, offices, and across the range of the labor force.[4]

Another source of labor came from the migration of southern whites to jobs in the North. Indiana received large numbers, drawn from Kentucky and further south by factories in Muncie, South Bend, and Gary. The newcomers were not always warmly received. Newspaper reporter John Bartlow Martin noted that a colleague told him: "Haven't you heard that there are only forty-five states left in the Union? Kentucky and Tennessee have gone to Indiana, and Indiana has gone to hell."[5]

WOMEN EMPLOYEES AT INDIANAPOLIS'S CONTINENTAL OPTICAL COMPANY WORK ON MATERIAL FOR THE WAR EFFORT AT THE FIRM'S PLANT ON NORTH CAPITOL AVENUE. IN RECOGNITION OF ITS OUTSTANDING SERVICES DURING THE CONFLICT, THE COMPANY RECEIVED THE PRESTIGIOUS ARMY-NAVY "E" AWARD WITH THREE STARS.

IHS, BRETZMAN COLLECTION, 21166-1

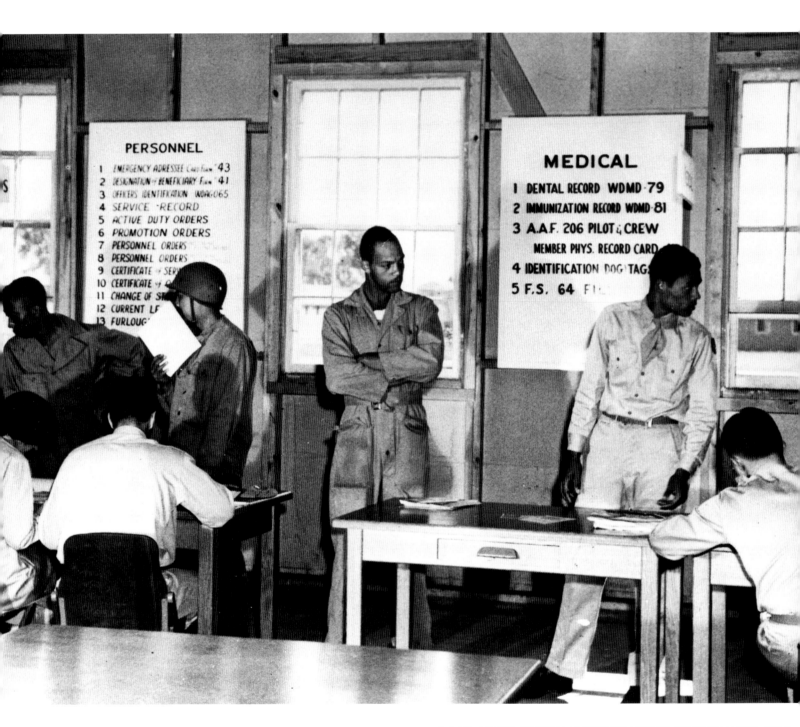

MEMBERS OF THE 320TH AVIATION SQUADRON ARRIVED AT FREEMAN FIELD NEAR SEYMOUR, INDIANA, ON JANUARY 21, 1943. THE SIX HUNDRED TROOPS PERFORMED SERVICE DUTIES AT THE AIRFIELD, THE SCENE OF A PROTEST BY AFRICAN-AMERICAN OFFICERS DENIED ACCESS TO THE BASE'S OFFICERS' CLUB ON ACCOUNT OF THEIR RACE.

INDIANA STATE ARCHIVES, INDIANA COMMISSION ON PUBLIC RECORDS

But the "hillbillies" were not at the bottom of the pile. That place white Americans reserved for black Americans. African-American workers had always found open only the lowest paid and least desirable jobs. Employers and labor unions resisted change at the start of the war, but growing shortages by 1943 forced hiring large numbers of black workers. Federal and state governments urged such changes, but nearly always in the cause of war victory rather than ideals of equality and justice. Conflicts between black and white workers flared, but in Indiana there was none of the extreme violence that happened elsewhere, most notably the Detroit riot of 1943. Still, African Americans faced discrimination everywhere and everyday, in restaurants, hotels, swimming pools, movie theaters, housing, and schools, as well as in wartime jobs. Although some whites (such as Indiana's Wendell Willkie) articulated the troubling irony of a racially segregated nation fighting against Nazism and its racist foundations, most white Americans chose not to see the contradictions until the civil rights movement of the 1950s and 1960s forced a hard look.[6]

Americans worked long hours to produce the massive quantities of weapons and materials that brought victory: airplanes and tanks, rifles and parachutes, K rations and boots, even soap and condoms. But home-front civilians made other sacrifices as well. From a global perspective those sacrifices were comparatively small, far smaller than the prices paid by the people of London, Dresden, Stalingrad, or Tokyo. American families lost loved ones, such as John Bushemi's family. But here too, in comparative statistical terms, the numbers were small: approximately 274,000 Americans died in World War II of the 50 million total deaths.[7] Individuals affected by personal loss seldom thought in such cold or abstract terms. The sacrifice of a brother's life or even the deprivation of a simple human comfort was a sacrifice. American sacrifices were real, and Americans made them in a cause they believed was just and necessary.

Americans who look back on the war almost always remember the sacrifices and the unity of purpose that propelled them. Rationing usually comes first in wartime memories, since more than others it affected daily life. At first glance, there was something un-American about not being able to buy whatever one wanted, and especially so after the depravations of the Great Depression. The necessities of war required that civilians give up freedom of consumption. A complicated system of rationing items needed for the military included gas rationing, with categories of need assigned to citizens. Those with lowest gasoline allocation had an "A" sticker pasted on their car windshield. One Evansville resident later recalled that those few

gallons his A sticker bought for his 1931 Chevrolet coupe weren't "enough for you to blow your nose at." With tire rationing added to the mix many Hoosiers gave up their cars. By 1943, visitors to Indiana's wonderful state parks were only a third the number of prewar 1941. And in the years from 1942 to 1945, no one drove to the Indiana State Fair or to the Indianapolis 500 because those celebrations were canceled for the duration. Even Eli Lilly had to carefully save his gas coupons in order to make a summer drive to Lake Wawasee.[8]

There was rationing and shortages of meat, sugar, coffee, butter, shoes, silk, and rubber items. Everyone planted a victory garden to supplement food supplies. Scrap drives collected newspaper, rubber, metal, and kitchen fat. In the spring of 1943, Hoosiers turned in the front license plates of their cars to be recycled to make the next year's back license plate. All the new plates would fit on old models, since the last new Studebaker, Chrysler, and Nash had rolled off assembly lines in early 1942. Housing shortages led to rent controls in towns such as Shelbyville, where the proximity to Camp Atterbury had sent rents skyrocketing. And for some there was the sacrifice brought by the new daylight savings time instituted in 1941 over strong opposition from workers, farmers, and others. Americans contributed financially by buying war bonds. Organized bond drives attracted massive support, enlisting Hollywood stars such as Carole Lombard, the Fort Wayne native who died tragically in a plane crash after an Indiana rally.[9]

The oft-expressed conviction in later years that this generation of Americans sacrificed and worked together as no generation had before or since has many exceptions and qualifications. Many Hoosiers found ways around some of the restrictions. They traded goods and ration stamps, and some used the black market to buy a nice cut of beef or a

THE OFT-EXPRESSED CONVICTION IN LATER YEARS THAT THIS GENERATION OF AMERICANS SACRIFICED AND WORKED TOGETHER AS NO GENERATION HAD BEFORE OR SINCE HAS MANY EXCEPTIONS AND QUALIFICATIONS.

TERRE HAUTE GROCER ERNEST ZWERNER CHECKS A CUSTOMER'S RATION BOOK. THE FEDERAL OFFICE OF PRICE ADMINISTRATION NOT ONLY ESTABLISHED PRICE CEILINGS TO PREVENT INFLATION, BUT ALSO INSTITUTED RATIONING ON SUCH SCARCE CONSUMER GOODS AS MEAT, SUGAR, COFFEE, TIRES, AND GASOLINE.
IHS, MARTIN COLLECTION

pound of sugar. Home-front civilians sometimes got cranky about rationing and sacrifice, particularly when they believed that they were sacrificing more than the next guy. Workers sometimes went on strike. Unions sometimes focused narrowly on growing their membership and power. Businessmen sometimes thought only of profit (and for those with government war contracts the profits did soar). As the war economy boomed, ordinary consumers had more money in their pockets and more opportunities than they had ever dreamed of, yet still talked of great sacrifice. Bored adolescents engaged in petty theft, premarital sex, and a surliness that identified them as teenagers with a special place in society. Their clothing, music, and slang offended elders, who began to label some of them as "juvenile delinquents." Quick military marriages, "goodbye babies," infidelity, and rising divorce rates challenged notions of stable family life. Prostitution and venereal diseases flourished on the home front and not far from the battlefront. Race continued to divide. Black soldiers on weekend passes in Indianapolis and other towns were denied rooms in hotels. More than a few factory workers quit a job rather than work alongside a black man or woman. In Muncie racism produced a near lynching in 1944.[10]

Americans did sacrifice—if not as ungrudgingly as they remembered decades later nor as fully as many citizens of other nations. The necessities of war required that they give up and make do for the duration. But for citizens in a democracy to accept the loss of life of loved ones as well as the freedom to drive their car or buy a nice roast they had to know why. Why should I fight? Why should I sacrifice?

Answers came from wartime news and propaganda, which shaped Americans' understanding of the war and also their memories of the war long after the peace of 1945. Who was the enemy? Why were the Axis powers dangerous to me? What could ordinary people

BUT FOR CITIZENS IN A DEMOCRACY TO ACCEPT THE LOSS OF LIFE OF LOVED ONES AS WELL AS THE FREEDOM TO DRIVE THEIR CAR OR BUY A NICE ROAST THEY HAD TO KNOW WHY. WHY SHOULD I FIGHT? WHY SHOULD I SACRIFICE?

PROPAGANDA POSTERS URGED AMERICAN CITIZENS TO DO WHAT THEY COULD TO HELP THE COUNTRY ACHIEVE VICTORY. HERE, A HOUSEWIFE SAVES TIRES AND GASOLINE BY CARRYING HER PURCHASES BACK HOME INSTEAD OF HAVING THEM DELIVERED.
INDIANA STATE ARCHIVES, COMMISSION ON PUBIC RECORDS

do to contribute to the enemy's defeat? What was this war about? What was the prospect for peace and for the future?

By answering these sacrifice questions, war news and propaganda met a fundamental necessity of war, that of raising and maintaining civilian morale. News and propaganda connected home-front citizens to the war so that they could imagine something of its nature, particularly so they could accept the challenges facing their husbands, brothers, and sons in uniform. If those in uniform were making sacrifices, surely we here at home must do our part. The stories and images of war were essential to home-front sacrifice and morale.

But citizens at home could know only part of the war. Even the best reporting could never capture its full and complex realities. And Americans were denied that full reporting because the news they received was carefully selected and presented in order to raise civilian morale. The U.S. government did commit to a "strategy of truth," that is, of not lying to citizens while still keeping necessary military secrets. Indiana's Elmer Davis, a respected radio broadcaster and head of the Office of War Information, was particularly keen to tell the American people as much about their war as possible. But the truth told was often only a part of the truth, skillfully selected, and seldom the whole truth. While it is likely that the federal govern-

ment's control of war news was less severe than that of any other combatant nation, American censorship and management of news was nonetheless careful and thorough in ways that often twisted the truth. In particular, Americans on the home front were spared most of the war's brutalities. They did not see the mangled bodies and the combat fatigue, as it was so gently labeled. They were spared too the ways in which young American males in uniform violated traditional notions of morality, evidenced in gambling, sexual promiscuity, venereal diseases, and massive consumption of alcohol. The soldiers whom home-front citizens read about or saw on film used cuss words such as "shucks" and "darn," never more salty ones, never the "f word," which was probably the most oft-used word of the war. The common acronym SNAFU, which was translated for home-front ears as "situation normal all fouled up," lost its power when the next to last word was cleaned up. Spared too from civilian eyes were the abundant examples of small and large SNAFUs all the way to the cases of "friendly fire" causing loss of American life. Loved ones at home saw little of the "chickenshit" and grumbling between officers and men and almost none of the racial disharmony in military camps and towns, such as the black officers' mutiny at Freeman Field near Seymour. Americans at home saw instead the heroic and clean side of war and only selected parts of the real war.[11]

The simplest but most important connection between war front and home front came in the mail. Letters were the personal link to a loved one overseas. Even though authorities censored letters from overseas they carried the personal news and feelings essential to home-front civilians, helping them understand something of the sacrifice of love ones. But letters usually told only part of the story because men writing home were careful to protect loved ones from the full reality of combat generally and particularly the realities of their own experiences of brutality, fear, or bitterness. Combat soldiers carefully sanitized their stories and often their feelings, perhaps especially in letters to women at home. When Private Myron Burkenpas of Lafayette described the horror of seeing a liberated German concentration camp he sent the letter to his father. In the last line he wrote: "Dad, it is for you to decide whether you want Mother and Dorothy to read this, but tell the boys at the shop what it is all about."[12]

Next to letters the most powerful words read at home were those from Ernie Pyle. All America knew the Hoosier reporter as this war's finest. His newspaper columns seemed to bring the real war closer to home. Few words ever written better captured the personal side of combat than Pyle's column on Captain Henry T. Waskow and the men who gathered in the Italian moonlight to say good-bye to their dead commander. Pyle tried to be upbeat, to show the comradeship, courage, and sacrifice of ordinary soldiers and to celebrate the efficiency and success of America's military machine. And he tried to be realistic in detailing the costs in hardship and in lives.

But as much as Pyle searched the keys on his Remington typewriter to describe the reality of combat, in the end he failed. He backed away from using his skills to describe the mangled bodies that were commonplace. Pyle chose not to tell his readers what Captain Waskow's wound looked like so as to leave his death "clean." And he chose not to describe fully the fatigue of mental breakdown or the incompetence or fear that led to needless deaths. Like other war correspondents Pyle left much untold because he knew Americans on the home front could not bear the truth. As playwright Arthur Miller concluded, Pyle "told as much of what he saw as people could read without vomiting." Even if he had been more willing to tell the whole truth and able also to bypass the military censors, his readers back home still would not have understood. He admitted so in a letter to General Dwight Eisenhower: "I think we're both fighting a losing cause—for I've found that no matter how much we talk, or write, or show pictures, people who have not actually been

they've got the GUTS

U.S. ARMY

GIVE 'EM MORE *FIREPOWER*

INDIANA HAD AN IMPRESSIVE LIST OF PRODUCTS ROLL OFF THE PRODUCTION LINE FOR USE BY TROOPS DURING THE WAR. EQUIPMENT INCLUDED AIRPLANE ENGINES, TRUCKS, BLOOD PLASMA, STEEL, PROXIMITY FUSES, CARTRIDGE CASES, SHELLS, TENT POLES, FIGHTER AIRCRAFT, AND LANDING CRAFT.

INDIANA STATE ARCHIVES, COMMISSION ON PUBLIC RECORDS

in war are incapable of having any real conception of it. I don't really blame the people.... I think I have helped make America conscious of and sympathetic toward [the infantryman], but I haven't made them *feel* what he goes through. I believe it's impossible. But I'll keep on trying."[13]

Pyle himself became increasingly numbed by the war's ongoing brutality. Tired and dispirited by the drive first through Italy and then from Normandy to Paris he nonetheless hauled himself off to the Pacific in early 1945. There a sniper's bullet ended his life. On his body, a column, unpublished and handwritten, became his legacy:

Dead men by mass production—in one country after another—month after month and year after year. Dead men in winter and dead men in summer. Dead men in such familiar promiscuity that they become monotonous. Dead men in such monstrous infinity that you come almost to hate them. Those are the things that you at home need not even try to understand. To you at home they are columns of figures, or he is a near one who went away and just didn't come back. You didn't see him lying so grotesque and pasty beside the gravel road in France. We saw him. Saw him by the multiple thousands. That's the difference.[14]

If Pyle's printed words were insufficient to convey the full truth of war they served the purpose of explaining the war in ways that home-front Americans could understand and support. So did the words that came from other reporters in newspaper and magazine stories and over the airwaves to radio sets in farmhouses and suburban cottages. War reporting convinced most Americans that this was a just and necessary war, that they did have to sacrifice, and that they did have a part to play even though their cities and factories were not bombed.[15]

Doubtless as important to civilian morale were the images that reached home-front eyes. In propaganda posters hanging in public libraries, factories, and post offices, government and industry urged workers to sacrifice and produce. "We can do it," the posters shouted. Magazine and newspaper advertisements carried messages that sold not only products such as toothpaste and makeup but sold also the war itself. Hollywood films explained the war, usually in propaganda that was easy to feel good about because they reaffirmed the essential goodness of America and Americans, as the film *Casablanca*, where even the seemingly selfish and isolationist Rick eventually does the right thing. Newsreels and film documentaries showed scenes of daily life and touches of combat in upbeat style, withholding images too depressing for home-front morale. Men who had actually experienced combat regarded film depictions with amusement and sometimes anger for their unrealistic and sanitized images of war.[16]

All these images were carefully selected and censored, likely even more so than the words of reporters. Government officials believed, for example, that pictures of dead GIs would harm civilian morale and thus kept them from the American people. When in late 1943 officials became concerned that citizens were becoming overconfident of imminent victory to the point of slacking off, they released carefully chosen photographs. Many on the home front only caught their first glimpse of a dead American soldier in September 1943, when *Life* magazine published George Strock's quiet photograph of three soldiers, their faces obscured, lying on the sands of Buna Beach in New Guinea. As the war reached its last months more and more photographs such as Strock's seeped out to the public because censors deemed them to be necessary motivational devices. All were carefully screened and selected. Images showing the worst horrors remained hidden long after the war was over. For home-front eyes American corpses, unlike Japanese, were always intact, the mortal wounds seldom visible. Other images were censored as well, such as those of a soldier showing fear or crying with emotion or exhaustion. Such brutal facts of war appear in all honest veterans' accounts of later years but not in photographs shown to the home front. Also deemed inappropriate for home-front unity and morale were photographs showing negative evidence of racial segregation within the military or black American soldiers mixing with white women in England or Italy.[17] John Bushemi's photographs were made and viewed in these contexts of sacrifice, hardship, and brutality, filtered by propaganda and censorship. Bushemi's photographs conveyed these themes from the

WHEN IN LATE 1943 OFFICIALS BECAME CONCERNED THAT CITIZENS WERE BECOMING OVERCONFIDENT OF IMMINENT VICTORY TO THE POINT OF SLACKING OFF, THEY RELEASED CAREFULLY CHOSEN PHOTOGRAPHS.

BODIES OF THREE DEAD AMERICAN SOLDIERS LYING IN THE SAND ON SHORELINE NEAR HALF-SUNKEN LANDING CRAFT ON BUNA BEACH AFTER A JAPANESE AMBUSH ATTACK.

GEORGE STROCK/TIME LIFE PICTURES/GETTY IMAGES

particular place of the Pacific theater, marked by sandy beaches, palm trees, and tropical breezes and by a harshness, savagery, and hatred that exceeded even that of Europe. Walter Goldsberry Jr., a marine from Greencastle, Indiana, captured the brutality of the war against Japan in a letter to his parents written in December 1943: "The Japs still own most of the real estate and are willing to die to hold it—and so they will. They're completely cut off. We admire the Japs for their tenacious fighting spirit, but we despise them for their resemblance to human beings."[18]

Among the most important features of the Pacific war was that neither side took many prisoners. For numerous reasons both Japanese and Americans fought to the death. Each was likely to kill enemy soldiers who attempted to surrender. At the end of the fighting on Tarawa, there were 4,700 Japanese dead and only 17 Japanese prisoners of war. Of course, Americans at home would never see a combat photographer's shot of an American killing an unarmed Japanese prisoner. Nor would they see the brutal souvenir hunting of a marine who extracted gold teeth from a wounded Japanese soldier, nor another marine urinating in the open mouth of a Japanese corpse. Such obscene images were unfit for home-front morale.[19]

The images and words that reached citizens at home in Indiana and across the nation inspired them to sacrifice, to give up leisurely auto drives to state parks and new shoes, to work longer hours, to do their part. But those same images that lifted home-front morale also left a selected, partial picture of the war. Most Americans were spared the brutality of war. They could only glimpse pieces of the real war in the Pacific and Europe. In not seeing this war Americans could come to believe it was a good war. And as the decades went by, their children and grandchildren became convinced as well, perhaps even more so. Paul Fussell, a thoughtful veteran who would have none of this good-war myth, wrote in 1989 that the war "has been sanitized and romanticized almost beyond recognition by the sentimental, the loony patriotic, the ignorant, and the bloodthirsty." To this bitter combat veteran "it was a war and nothing else, and thus stupid and sadistic."[20]

Veterans came home in 1945 and focused on family, work, and play, as they embarked on the greatest period of long-term economic prosperity the United States has ever known. From those who fought this war, who really knew it firsthand, whose hearts and heads were filled with sad memories, there was mostly silence in the decades that followed. Many of them, such as former combat medic Bernard Rice of Mishawaka, seldom talked about the war and kept their nightmares mostly to themselves: "For the first thirty-five years after the war, I tried desperately to forget," Rice wrote in

1997, adding "I was only partially successful; there was much that refused to be forgotten." It took Kurt Vonnegut twenty-four years to share his memory of the slaughterhouse in which he survived the Dresden firestorm. It took E. B. Sledge, a Marine veteran of Peleliu and Okinawa, more than three decades to tell his story of the "meat grinder."[21]

The best accounts and memories of veterans open possibilities of seeing more of what they saw and of seeing what those on the wartime home front did not see. These fuller, more honest accounts differ from news received on the wartime home front. Many veterans' memories tend to be less heroic and celebratory, particularly when removed from Memorial Day or Veterans Day ceremonies. They show the courage and heroism of war, though often modestly, and they reinforce the knowledge that this was a war that had to be won. But they also leave no doubt that it was a nasty and brutal war.

The timing here is critical. In the vacuum of silence after 1945 the myth of the good war grew, especially in the 1960s and 1970s, when another war, so different, became the "bad war."[22] America's story of World War II became a triumphal and one-sided story. Stories that did not fit this good war narrative stayed on back burners, from the Japanese-American internment at home to the fire bombings of Dresden and Tokyo, to the critical role played by American Allies, particularly the Soviet Union (there was always some room for Great Britain in America's triumph, since "we bailed them out"). With the fiftieth anniversary that began on December 7, 1991, this good war narrative came to full bloom.

Americans will always want to believe in the good war. How else to justify such loss? But in the twenty-first century a fuller and more honest picture of the war is emerging, one more ambiguous and complex. It is a picture of war that leaves no doubt that this was a just and necessary war, a war that America had to fight and had to win. It is a picture that leaves no doubt that victory was marked by courage and sacrifice, including the kind that John Bushemi so nobly made. But it is an understanding of this war that is fuller and more complete, more honest, more able to include the bad and the good, and especially the in-between, the shades of gray, the ambiguities and complexities that are at the center of war and all human activity.

James H. Madison is Thomas and Kathryn Miller professor of history at Indiana University, Bloomington. He is the editor of World War II: A History in Documents, *which is forthcoming from Oxford University Press. He is also the author of* A Lynching in the Heartland: Race and Memory in America *(2001);* Eli Lilly: A Life, 1885–1977 *(1989); and* The Indiana Way: A State History *(1986).*

JOHN A. BUSHEMI

A BIOGRAPHY RAY E. BOOMHOWER

On February 19, 1944, two battalions of the U.S. Army's 106th Infantry, Twenty-seventh Division, hit the beaches of Eniwetok Island, part of the Eniwetok atoll located at the far northwest end of the Marshall Islands in the central Pacific. As the American soldiers crept toward their objectives, they were continually sniped at from the side and rear by Japanese troops cleverly hidden in a series of camouflaged foxholes and trenches. Observing the operation that day were two men—a correspondent and a photographer—from *Yank*, the army's weekly magazine produced by and written for enlisted men. As the correspondent, Merle Miller, and other combat journalists stopped about

seventy-five yards behind the front lines to examine a bullet-riddled chest of books, they became targets for a series of Japanese knee-mortar shells. Shrapnel from the shells hit and mortally wounded Miller's companion, Staff Sergeant John A. Bushemi, who before the war had worked as a photographer for the *Gary Post-Tribune*. Bushemi's first concern after being hit was not for his wounds but for his camera equipment. As Navy surgeons frantically attempted to save the photographer's life onboard a transport, Bushemi, with his last words, said to Miller: "Be sure to get those pictures back to the office."[1]

Before his fatal wounding on Eniwetok, Bushemi, who had earned the nickname "One Shot" during his work with the Gary newspaper for his uncanny ability to capture even the liveliest action with just one click of his shutter, had participated in numerous landings in the Pacific theater. Even a hand injury suffered during the invasion of the Kwajalein atoll that left his arm in a sling had not stopped Bushemi from documenting for *Yank*'s readers the achievements gained and agonies endured by their fellow soldiers. Miller, a noted novelist and

PREVIOUS PAGES: WITH HIS MOVIE CAMERA SLUNG OVER HIS LEFT SHOULDER, BUSHEMI PREPARES TO CAPTURE THE ACTION ON ENIWETOK ISLAND FOR *YANK*.

MARY ELLEN CESSNA

OPPOSITE: A CANDID SHOT OF BUSHEMI DURING HIS DAYS AT THE *GARY POST-TRIBUNE*. THE WEDDING RING HE WEARS ON HIS LEFT HAND BELONGED TO HIS LATE MOTHER, ANGELINA.

CALUMET REGIONAL ARCHIVES, INDIANA UNIVERSITY NORTHWEST

historian after the war, said his partner specialized in "photography from a rifle's length vantage point." Although Bushemi's duties, which included taking still photographs and shooting movies, did not require him to go into actual combat, Miller said, the photographer did so anyway, becoming the second of four *Yank* staff members killed during the war.[2] His work with his ubiquitous Speed Graphic camera earned for Bushemi the distinction of being "*Yank*'s most outstanding combat photographer," noted Joe McCarthy, the magazine's managing editor. In addition to admiring Bushemi's photographs, McCarthy said that other staff members at the magazine also appreciated "his good-natured sincerity and devotion to his work, which made friends for him and increased the prestige of *Yank* in every camp and theater of operation that he visited."[3]

The seventh of nine children of parents who had emigrated from Sicily to the United States, Bushemi, described by his friends at the *Post-Tribune* as "a dapper, darkly handsome youth whose ready quip and irresistible grin were never to be denied," received numerous honors immediately after his death.[4] In addition to being awarded a posthumous Bronze Star and a Purple Heart by the U.S. government, the photographer received a correspondent's valor medal from the National Headliners Club and was inducted into the News Photographers Hall of Fame at the Memorial Press Center in New York City in 1944. Two years later the Veterans of Foreign Wars named a post in Gary for Bushemi, and the Indiana Associated Press named its award for the best news photograph of the year after him. In 1957 a U.S. Army Reserve Training Center opened in Gary and was dedicated in Bushemi's memory. The photographer's vibrant and daring personality, noted Calumet Region historian James B. Lane, caused Gary residents to consider him as their representative soldier of

IN APRIL 2001 BUSHEMI WAS INDUCTED INTO THE INDIANA JOURNALISM HALL OF FAME. . . . ALL OF THIS ADULATION MIGHT HAVE EMBARRASSED BUSHEMI, A PERFECTIONIST WHO NEVER SEEMED TO BELIEVE HIS PHOTOGRAPHS WERE QUITE GOOD ENOUGH.

BUSHEMI DIRECTS TRAFFIC FOR A SHOT DURING HIS COVERAGE FOR *YANK* OF ARMY DESERT WARFARE TRAINING IN CALIFORNIA IN 1942.
MARY ELLEN CESSNA

**BOXING IN GOLDEN GLOVES
TOURNAMENTS AND OFFERING
HAIRCUTS TO NEIGHBORHOOD
YOUTHS HELPED BUSHEMI EARN
SOME MONEY DURING THE HEIGHT
OF THE GREAT DEPRESSION.**

MARY ELLEN CESSNA

World War II over the likes of such local notables as football star Tom Harmon and boxing champion Tony Zale. During the war, Bushemi served as the inspiration for a regular column in the *Post-Tribune* called "Dear Johnny," which offered soldiers overseas reports on what was happening back home.[5] In April 2001 Bushemi was inducted into the Indiana Journalism Hall of Fame, which since its creation in 1966 by the Indiana chapter of the Society of Professional Journalists, Sigma Delta Chi, has honored Hoosier journalists of distinction.[6]

All of this adulation might have embarrassed Bushemi, a perfectionist who never seemed to believe his photographs were quite good enough; this despite the fact his work appeared in the *Saturday Evening Post* and *New York Times Magazine.* Writing to his youngest sister, Mary Ellen, about his experiences on Guadalcanal, Bushemi said he was "disgusted" with the quality of his work, which included shooting a short motion picture of Eleanor Roosevelt's visit to the island—this despite the fact that Roosevelt was so pleased with the efforts that she used the production to entertain friends at the White House. "You might be interested in knowing that during the time, I enjoyed shooting 500 feet of front line operations in New Georgia," he wrote, "which also was lousy. The office is using it, but that really doesn't make me satisfied."[7] Later, after he had left the relatively routine invasion of Makin in the Gilbert Islands to photograph the aftermath of the bloody battle at Tarawa, Bushemi wrote Sergeant Leo Hofeller, *Yank*'s picture editor, expressing his dissatisfaction with his work. "I'm sorry as hell about not giving you better stuff on Tarawa," he wrote Hofeller. "I feel I've let you guys down."[8]

Photography as a means of earning a living was a novelty for the Buscemi family (Americanized to Bushemi in the early 1930s). The family's patriarch, Pietro, a native of Calascibetta, Sicily, left his pregnant wife and son in Villarosa, Sicily, for America aboard the *Prinz Oscar* in May 1906. Landing at New York City on June 2, 1906, Pietro traveled to Kansas City, Missouri, to join his uncle, Liborio Vetri. Eventually settling in Centerville, Iowa, Pietro was joined there by his wife, Angelina Cariota, and the couple's son Mario and daughter Vincenzina in 1909. While Pietro toiled in a local coal mine, his wife worked in the family-owned Bluebird Café. John was born in Centerville on April 19, 1917. The children numbered six boys and three girls when in 1925 the family moved to Taylorville, Illinois, where Pietro worked for the Peabody Coal Company. Four years later, with the Great Depression tightening its grip on the nation's economy, including the coal industry, Pietro heard from relatives that there might be jobs available in the steel mills of Gary, Indiana. The entire Bushemi family moved to the Hoosier State in May 1930, settling in Gary's Glen Park neighborhood, and Pietro found a job in U.S. Steel's coke plant.[9]

As a teenager growing up during the Great Depression, John Bushemi did whatever he could to earn money, from boxing in Golden Gloves tournaments to offering haircuts for twenty-five cents from a barber's chair bought for him by his father and located in the basement of the family's home at 3927 Monroe Street (the Bushemis moved to 3500 Connecticut Street in 1936, which would remain in the family for the next thirty-five years). Unfortunately for Bushemi, his haircutting skills soon attracted the attention of the neighborhood's barber, who noticed a steady decline in his regular customers, noted Mary Ellen. Local authorities soon put an end to Bushemi's unlicensed operation. Although he was tempted to skirt local regulations, Bushemi faced the stern disapproval of his mother, Angelina. "She said, 'No way, we're not having any problems [with the law],'" said Mary Ellen. After he quit school before his junior year at Gary's Lew

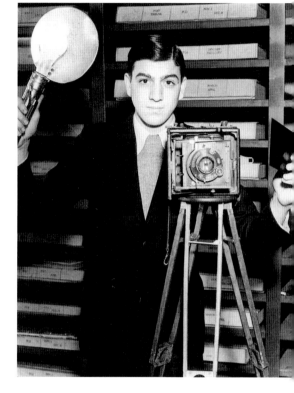

BUSHEMI AS A YOUNG APPRENTICE PHOTOGRAPHER ON THE *GARY POST-TRIBUNE.*
DEPAUW UNIVERSITY ARCHIVES AND SPECIAL COLLECTIONS

Wallace High School, Bushemi joined his father and brothers in working at the local steel mills. "He wanted to go to work and buy a camera," said Mary Ellen. "That's what he wanted to do—he wanted to take pictures." With the wages from his job he purchased his first camera, a small Univex that he used to snap photographs of family members and special occasions. He developed the film in a darkroom located in a closet in the family's home. "With that little camera, you knew that someday he would be a photographer," Mary Ellen noted.[10]

Tragedy struck the Bushemi family on August 31, 1935, when its matriarch, Angelina, died of cancer. After a wake in the family home and a funeral at St. Mark Catholic Church, her body was taken to Centerville, Iowa, where she was buried in Oakland Cemetery. While the rest of the family returned to Gary, John Bushemi stayed behind in Centerville for several weeks. For the rest of his life, he wore his mother's wedding ring in honor of her memory.[11] With his mother's death, Bushemi shouldered additional responsibilities at home, becoming particularly close with Mary Ellen, who often waited for her brother on the back step of the family's home until he returned late at night from his assignments for the *Post-Tribune*. Taking his sibling inside, Bushemi tucked her into bed and stayed with her until she finally fell asleep. Mary Ellen used to visit her brother at the newspaper's offices at Fourth Avenue and Broadway whenever she was downtown and even accompanied him on his safer assignments, particularly sporting events. "He always had that big smile," she remembered. "He was a happy person because he loved his job." After joining the service, Bushemi continued to look after Mary Ellen, sending her photographs of the movie stars—Dinah Shore, Veronica Lake, Mickey Rooney—who visited his army base and making sure she received a subscription to *Yank* when he joined the staff there.[12]

ALTHOUGH BUSHEMI COVERED A VARIETY OF COMMUNITY EVENTS FOR THE *POST-TRIBUNE*, HE EARNED HIS REPUTATION TAKING SPORTS PHOTOGRAPHS, WHERE HIS "PERFECT TIMING" CAPTURED ATHLETES AT THEIR BEST.

PHOTOGRAPHERS FOR THE *POST-TRIBUNE* EXAMINE SOME OF THEIR WORK. PICTURED FROM LEFT TO RIGHT ARE ELMER BUDLOVE, CHARLES SMITH, BUSHEMI, AND HERB LUKMANN.

MARY ELLEN CESSNA

On June 24, 1936, Bushemi left the steel mills for good when the *Post-Tribune* hired him as an apprentice photographer. Earlier, he had struck up a friendship with Franz Allebach, the newspaper's first photographer. While still in high school Bushemi had sometimes assisted Allebach in order to learn more about photojournalism.[13] Although Bushemi covered a variety of community events for the *Post-Tribune*, he earned his reputation taking sports photographs, where his "perfect timing" captured athletes at their best. He won numerous awards for his sports photography in contests sponsored by the Indiana Associated Press and the Inland Daily Press Association, which included entrants from newspapers published in eighteen states. Reflecting on Bushemi's career following his death, however, the *Post-Tribune* noted that the photographer's real talent lay in shooting quieter settings—"snow scenes, dunes reeds etching their scrolls in the sands, rippled dunes with poplars bending above."[14]

The photographer's skill at capturing bucolic nature scenes belied his sometimes intrepid character, particularly when it came to covering crime during his five years on the newspaper. "He liked adventure," said Mary Ellen, noting that her brother took numerous chances to get crime photographs.[15] Tom Nestler, whose family had also moved from Centerville, Iowa, to Gary, called his longtime friend a daredevil, noting, "He did things no one else would do." Nestler, who sometimes assisted Bushemi on his assignments, remembered one occasion when Bushemi showed up at his door late one night seeking his help in covering a robbery at a gambling club on Gary's Ridge Road. Hiding behind some convenient trees, the duo caught the thief climbing down a telephone pole. Their hiding place, however, could not obscure the sound and light from Bushemi's flash. "This guy has a gun pointing at Johnny," Nestler recalled, but the duo escaped

TOM NESTLER CALLED HIS LONGTIME FRIEND A DAREDEVIL, NOTING, "HE DID THINGS NO ONE ELSE WOULD DO." BUSHEMI'S DEDICATION TO HIS WORK EVEN SURVIVED A VICIOUS ASSAULT FROM AN ANGRY RAILROAD DETECTIVE.

FROM HIS DAYS ON THE *POST-TRIBUNE* TO HIS WORK FOR *YANK*, BUSHEMI DISPLAYED A "WARMTH AND ENERGY AND FRIENDLINESS TO AND FOR EVERYONE HE MET," ACCORDING TO HIS FRIEND AND COLLEAGUE MERLE MILLER.
DEPAUW UNIVERSITY ARCHIVES AND SPECIAL COLLECTIONS

unharmed. "Johnny was just one of a kind," he added.[16]

Bushemi's dedication to his work even survived a vicious assault from an angry railroad detective. Assigned to cover the wreck of a New York Central Railroad freight train, which had derailed just west of Chesterton's business district late one Saturday evening, Bushemi had begun to take photographs of a smashed boxcar while standing in Railroad Park, a property leased to the City of Chesterton by New York Central. Suddenly, an unidentified uniformed officer grabbed Bushemi, ordered him to stop taking pictures, and told him to "get the _____ out of here." The 135-pound photographer was next confronted by a plainclothes railroad detective, later identified as Henry O'Heim of La Porte. The 200-pound O'Heim grabbed Bushemi and threatened to knock his block off. Asked by Bushemi to identify himself, O'Heim responded by pushing the photographer two hundred feet through the park to State Road 49, all the while kicking and beating on the photographer with his fists. When the two reached the road, Bushemi placed his camera and supply case on the curb and O'Heim attacked both of them with his feet, smashing them into pieces.

Discussing the incident with a *Post-Tribune* reporter, Bushemi noted, "I had no way of knowing he [O'Heim] was a railroad policeman, since he wouldn't identify himself. Besides, I wasn't on railroad property, either when I took my first and only picture or when he smashed my camera." Undeterred by the assault, Bushemi grabbed another camera and continued to photograph the train wreck, this time unmolested by the railroad lawmen. At the request of the *Post-Tribune*, Charles T. Allen, Chesterton justice of the peace, swore out a warrant accusing O'Heim of assault. The charges were later withdrawn by the newspaper after the detective went to the *Post-Tribune*'s offices to formally apologize to Bushemi. Also, New York Central Railroad officials, who had reprimanded O'Heim for the incident, expressed their regret to Bushemi and paid to replace his watch and camera equipment broken during the assault.[17]

Just five months before the American Pacific fleet was attacked by the Japanese at Pearl Harbor on December 7, 1941, Bushemi received his draft notice for the U.S. Army, becoming the first *Post-Tribune* staff member to enter military service. (Two of Bushemi's brothers also served during the war—Joe with the army's 135th Medical Regiment and Sam with the marines as a photographer.) After his induction and testing at the new reception center at Fort Benjamin Harrison in Indianapolis in July 1941, Bushemi—army serial number 35164228—traveled to the

BUSHEMI SHAKES HANDS WITH HIS BROTHER JOE, ON LEAVE FROM CAMP SHELBY, MISSISSIPPI, AS HE PREPARES TO LEAVE WITH FORTY-FIVE OTHER YOUNG MEN FROM GARY FOR INDUCTION INTO THE ARMY AT INDIANAPOLIS'S FORT BENJAMIN HARRISON. LOOKING ON IS ANOTHER INDUCTEE, GEORGE TICHAC.

GARY POST-TRIBUNE

**A SHOT OF MARION HARGROVE TAKEN
BY BUSHEMI AND USED FOR PUBLICITY
FOR HARGROVE'S BEST-SELLING BOOK
SEE HERE, PRIVATE HARGROVE.
MANY OF THE PIECES IN THE BOOK
WERE FIRST PRINTED AS COLUMNS
IN THE *CHARLOTTE NEWS.***

MARY ELLEN CESSNA

Field Artillery Replacement Center at Fort Bragg in North Carolina for basic training.[18] Before long, however, the army realized that Bushemi's true skills lay not in firing a 75-mm gun but in shooting a camera. Officers assigned him to the public relations office for the Field Artillery Replacement Center, which was staffed by three privates: Don Bishop, Thomas James Montgomery Mulvehill, and Marion Hargrove. "Army life was quite pleasant in those days," remembered Hargrove, who had worked for the *Charlotte News* in civilian life and who wrote about his experiences in the army in a column for the newspaper. "It was peaceful and quiet, devoid of tension or overwork, and war was the farthest thought from the average soldier's mind." The only item that disturbed the calm, he added, was the extension of the draft term from twelve to thirty months. "The working week always ended at 10:30 on Saturday morning," said Hargrove, "at which time the Army got into civilian clothes and took off."[19]

Until Bushemi joined the public relations staff, said Hargrove, the three privates had been used to a leisurely pace, writing articles about soldiers at the base for hometown newspapers. "All of our stories were about corporals promoted to sergeants and parents and girlfriends visiting at the guesthouse," he remembered. Hargrove, who had been first assigned as an army cook, admitted that he never did "an honest day's work in the Army" until he teamed with Bushemi. "I liked him from the moment I saw him," Hargrove said of Bushemi. "Everyone just loved Bush. He was a charming guy, a hard worker, [and] a good photographer." Bringing with him, as he did, "the faint whiff of photographic hypo," Bushemi never had an idle minute from the moment he reported for duty, possessed as he was with "an unfailing energy and an unfailing sense of humor," said Hargrove.[20]

The first day he came to work for the office Bushemi teamed with Hargrove to cover the annual mile-and-a-quarter obstacle race involving the base's Fourth Training Regiment. If he had been the photographer, Hargrove said he would have napped on the sidelines until the event finished and then snapped a picture of the winner as he received the $25 defense bond prize from the regimental commander. Bushemi took a quite different approach. To obtain a picture of the race's start, Bushemi climbed on top of a large platform. When the race started, Hargrove said, the photographer jumped from the platform and, fully loaded with camera and equipment, ran down the course to follow the participants. Photographing his way through the obstacles, Bushemi almost managed to keep pace with the racers. The winner finished the course, panting heavily, in about six minutes, said Hargrove, with the second, third, and fourth place finishers coming in out of breath right before Bushemi showed up, "fresh and nonchalant." The photographer apologized to Hargrove for missing the finish, saying, "I guess my wind ain't as good as it once was." If Bushemi had not been hampered by the weight of his camera equipment, Hargrove predicted, the photographer might have won the race. Bushemi displayed the same dedication to his job a week later when he photographed 155-mm "Long Tom" guns in action on the base's firing range. Although the crews ran for cover to escape the noise and concussion when the guns were fired, Hargrove noted that Bushemi, "with wads of cotton hanging loosely from his ears," stood only three feet from the artillery and captured every blast on film.[21]

The energy displayed by Bushemi on the obstacle course and firing range, however, was not evident most mornings when reveille sounded at six o'clock. It was the public relations staff's "first and hardest job of the day" to get Bushemi out of bed in time for morning

BUSHEMI AND HARGROVE DEVELOPED A CLOSE AND JOKING FRIENDSHIP DURING THEIR ARMY DAYS. ON ONE OCCASION, HARGROVE PLAYFULLY BEQUEATHED TO HIS FRIEND "THE SOLE RESPONSIBILITY AND CARE OF THE PUBLIC RELATIONS OFFICE . . . TO HAVE AND TO HOLD, TO LOVE AND TO CHERISH" FOR EXACTLY ONE DAY.
MARY ELLEN CESSNA

BUSHEMI AND AN UNIDENTIFIED DRIVER PROWL THE GROUNDS AT FORT BRAGG
LOOKING FOR ANY NEWS THAT MIGHT INTEREST THE BASE'S PUBLIC RELATIONS STAFF.
BUSHEMI SIGNED THIS PHOTOGRAPH FOR HIS SISTER MARY ELLEN ON DECEMBER 6,
1941, A DAY BEFORE THE JAPANESE STRUCK THE AMERICAN FLEET AT PEARL HARBOR.

MARY ELLEN CESSNA

roll call, said Hargrove. Every daybreak without fail Hargrove, Bishop, and Mulvehill would gather near the photographer's bunk and scream at him for three minutes to get out of bed. "This evoked a few muffled and bitter snarls from beneath Bushemi's blankets," Hargrove said. The routine—termed "an ordeal" by Hargrove—ended with one of the three privates placing his foot in the small of Bushemi's back and rolling him out of bed. Standing in front of the barracks in the cold and dark with the other soldiers, Bushemi would "sound out awake and cheerful" when his name was called out during roll call, said Hargrove. His squad mates might not have known that Bushemi was clad only in shoes, pants, an overcoat, and cap. Immediately after dismissal from roll call, Bushemi always returned to the comfort of his bunk and slept until it was time to go to work. "He never had an official army breakfast in his life," Hargrove said of his friend.[22]

Although Bushemi was devoted to his duties (Hargrove noted that the photographer was "a maniac for work"), he nevertheless found time to charm his fellow soldiers, and their girlfriends as well. "I don't think I've ever known a more thoroughly likeable and ingratiating person than Bushemi," said Hargrove. "His personality was that of a young and frisky puppy, full of friendliness and genuine charm." In the public relations office,

Mulvehill had always been credited as the smoothest operator of the bunch, particularly when it came to ambitious schemes. Still, Hargrove recalled that on occasion he witnessed Mulvehill approach Bushemi with the intention of borrowing fifty cents only to end up lending the photographer a dollar. Hoping to keep his friend from feeling homesick, Hargrove took Bushemi with him on a visit back home to Charlotte. Within a week, Hargrove said, Bushemi had completely taken over the town. "When we entered the *News* office together," Hargrove noted in *See Here, Private Hargrove*, "everybody greeted Bushemi with a hearty hand and me with a causal nod." It became too much for Hargrove when Bushemi began inviting him on trips to Charlotte, working his magic on the girl Hargrove had been seeing, and even offering to find his lonely friend a date. (Bushemi's female friends in Gary later dubbed him "The Don Juan of Fort Bragg.") "There is nothing left there for me," Hargrove said of his hometown. "It's Bushemi territory. If I ever get a furlough again, I'll probably have to go to Gary, Indiana."[23]

Although sometimes rivals when it came to available women, Hargrove did all he could to promote Bushemi's work, including trying his own hand at photography. When the base's commanding officer, Edwin P. Parker Jr., received his promotion from colonel to brigadier general, Bushemi had the assignment to photograph Hargrove interviewing Parker. "Then, we decided, it was only fair that I photograph Bushemi photographing the General," said Hargrove, who sent the image to the *Gary Post-Tribune*. Later, during a Bushemi photo shoot involving 155-mm artillery, Hargrove again volunteered to take a picture of the photographer in action for the Gary newspaper. Apart from nearly being blown over backwards by blasts from the heavy guns, Hargrove said he did "fairly well" with the camera. When the duo returned to the public relations office, they were met, after Hargrove's photo had been printed, with laughter by others in the department who were becoming used to the routine of Hargrove snapping a photograph of Bushemi while he was shooting something else. Hargrove quoted Bushemi as noting: "Man, if you think that's good, just wait until we get another photographer. His only job will be taking pictures of Hargrove taking pictures of Bushemi taking pictures of the original photographer taking pictures of Hargrove. That is, until the Captain decides to get an entire new staff."[24]

In early March 1942 Fort Bragg received a visit from a distinguished guest: Pulitzer Prize–winning playwright Maxwell Anderson, who came to the camp to gather material for a war play he planned on writing, which eventually became *The Eve of St. Mark*. After visiting with General Parker, Anderson wandered around the base and happened to see a "tall, good looking soldier" (Hargrove) being fleeced of his money by a group of his buddies (Mulvehill, Bushemi, and Maury Sher). "This, suh," Anderson quoted Hargrove as saying, "is my holding company, making a division of my monthly pay." Bushemi explained to Anderson that three times a year Hargrove became indebted to his friends in order to raise needed funds for trips to visit his girlfriend. If his friends refused to lend him the money for such excursions, Hargrove could not write, said Bushemi, and if he experienced writer's block "we haven't got a prayer of getting our money back. You see, we're pretty deep in." Intrigued, Anderson asked to see Hargrove's work. Impressed by the comic writing style, the playwright later passed the manuscript on to his neighbor, William M. Sloane III, an editor at Henry Holt and Company. "The writing is amusing and imaginative," Anderson wrote Sloane, "yet the author sticks to reality enough to give a fairly accurate notion of what it's like to be inducted." In July 1942 Henry Holt and Company published the columns in the book *See Here, Private Hargrove*, which became a best-seller and subsequently a movie. (Bushemi provided publicity photographs of Hargrove for the book, including one of the author for the back cover.)[25]

PLAYWRIGHT MAXWELL ANDERSON (LEFT) VISITS WITH FORT BRAGG'S COMMANDING OFFICER EDWIN P. PARKER JR. (FAR RIGHT) AND AN UNIDENTIFIED OFFICER IN THE GENERAL'S OFFICE AT THE BASE. ANDERSON WROTE AT THE TOP OF THE PHOTO: "HELL, I'M CERTAINLY IN GOOD LOOKING COMPANY."

MARY ELLEN CESSNA

Hargrove, who served as Anderson's guide during his visit to the army base, said that the famous author proved to be "so remarkably (and astonishingly) congenial and charming" that his fellow soldiers were more than happy to help him with his research. Although Anderson had come to Fort Bragg downhearted due to the dire war news and the recent death in an airplane accident of his favorite nephew, Staff Sargent Lee Chambers, the playwright's introduction to the lively group of soldiers "visibly inspirited" him, noted Hargrove, and also encouraged him "about the future of the war and the materials he had already put together for his play." In addition to Hargrove, Bushemi, and Sher, Anderson also received insights on the soldiers' lives from Private Lloyd Shearer, who worked at the main base's public relations operation and also produced freelance articles for various magazines and newspapers. On Sunday, March 8, 1942, Anderson, joined by Hargrove, Bushemi, and Shearer (known as Skip to his friends), visited Chapel Hill, North Carolina, for a lunch at the home of Paul Green, a playwright then teaching at the University of North Carolina, followed by a meeting with drama students.[26]

As the weary group traveled back to Fort Bragg late Sunday evening, somebody suggested that instead of taking Anderson back to his hotel room in Fayetteville, only to be brought back to the base in a few hours, the playwright should instead spend the night in the barracks. "That would not only give Max at least an extra hour of sleep, but would also expose him to the eloquent and blasphemous language of citizen soldiery roused out of its bed in the morning," said Hargrove. Shearer returned to the main post as Hargrove and Bushemi found a bed for their guest. "Bushemi gave him [Anderson] his own bunk, between mine and Bishop's, and slept in a vacant bunk nearby," said Hargrove, adding that Mulvehill returned about the same

"THE WRITING IS AMUSING AND IMAGINATIVE," ANDERSON WROTE . . . "YET THE AUTHOR STICKS TO REALITY ENOUGH TO GIVE A FAIRLY ACCURATE NOTION OF WHAT IT'S LIKE TO BE INDUCTED." IN JULY 1942 HENRY HOLT AND COMPANY PUBLISHED THE COLUMNS IN THE BOOK *SEE HERE, PRIVATE HARGROVE*, WHICH BECAME A BEST-SELLER.

BUSHEMI REVIEWS A COPY OF *SEE HERE, PRIVATE HARGROVE* WITH THE BOOK'S AUTHOR. "THAT MARVELOUS BOOK ILLUMINATED—AND ILLUMINATES EVEN TODAY—THAT TIME OF OUR LIVES," SAID EARL HAMNER JR., CREATOR OF *THE WALTONS* AND A LONGTIME HARGROVE FRIEND.
MARY ELLEN CESSNA

time they had. The only regular missing from the barracks was Bishop, who spent his weekends at his home in Washington, North Carolina. What the group had forgotten, however, was the daily routine they used to wake Bushemi in time for reveille. At six o'clock on Monday morning, when there were no signs of life from the beds, Bishop began shouting at what he thought was Bushemi: "Get the hell out of that sack! Get up, get up, get up!" Getting no response, Bishop responded by shaking the bed and was about to use his foot to shove the supposed sleeping Bushemi from his warm bed, Hargrove noted, when Anderson appeared from beneath the covers. Hargrove noted that a surprised Bishop responded by saying: "Oh, *hi*, Max. Didn't know *you* were here." In all the confusion, Bushemi slumbered peacefully nearby; nobody had remembered to wake him up in time for reveille.[27]

Anderson displayed no animus for his unusual awakening. After the incident in the barracks, he jokingly told the soldiers that he would write them into one of his future plays, "maybe as grave diggers," said Anderson.[28] On March 11, 1942, the playwright wrote Parker at Fort Bragg offering to repay the hospitality shown him at the camp by writing a half-hour comedy skit about life in the barracks at reveille that could be used to entertain the troops at bases around the country. Anderson

asked the general for permission to send Hargrove to New York City to help him prepare such a script. "I shall try to write it whether I can get help or not, but one of the men who slept in the same barracks and knows all the procedure, could certainly add to the local color," Anderson noted. Parker agreed to Anderson's request and, a few weeks later, Hargrove received leave and journeyed north to supposedly help produce what became a skit titled "From Reveille to Breakfast," which had Fort Bragg as its locale. In fact, Hargrove later told Anderson's biographer Alfred Shivers that he had played no role in writing the skit.[29]

The "local color" referred to by Anderson surfaced again in the playwright's next production, the aforementioned *The Eve of St. Mark*, which opened to rave reviews at New York's Cort Theatre on October 7, 1942, and ran for three hundred and seven performances, becoming, as one Anderson biographer has noted, one of the playwright's most popular works.[30] At the time Anderson had consulted Shearer, Bushemi, and Hargrove about army life, and bought them some steak dinners in Fayetteville, the soldiers believed that Anderson was merely "making a philanthropic and meaty contribution to our sorely tired soldier stomachs," said Shearer. The men were unaware that they and the restaurant they ate and drank beer at (the Rainbow Grill) would be featured in Anderson's new play as the Moonbow Restaurant. About six months after Anderson's visit to Fort Bragg, the soldiers attended a rehearsal of his new play in New York and found "three actors on the stage, imitating us—not as the promised grave diggers, but as three soldiers at Fort Bragg," Shearer indignantly reported in "Pertaining to Local Color," an article he wrote for the *New York Times*. "Mr. Anderson had not even bothered to change some of our names. There we were, alive, in his play."[31]

Of course, as in any production, Shearer said that Anderson had taken some "poetic license" with the stories of the real-life characters. For example, the actor who served as the prototype for Hargrove was shown actually firing an artillery piece. The closest Hargrove had ever been to such a gun, Shearer claimed, only happened "when, through a window, he watched a gun being rolled down the road." Also, Anderson had one of the soldiers resisting the charms of a comely blonde female: "This, I am certain," said Shearer, "does not pertain to any of us." The actors were surprised to learn that they were "portraying live soldiers," examining the men as if they "were freaks from some far-off land." When the trio asked about the resemblances between the fictional soldiers on stage and real-life people at Fort Bragg (character names included Private Francis Marion, described in notes for the plays as "a handsome Southerner,

with equally handsome manners"; Private Thomas Mulveroy; Private Shevlin; and Private Buscemi), the play's manager told them that any similarity with actual persons, living or dead, was purely coincidental. "I looked at Corporal Hargrove," Shearer wrote. "Corporal Hargrove looked at Sergeant Bushemi. And Sergeant Bushemi looked at me. 'Baloney!' we said." Before leaving the theater, the soldiers left a joking warning for Anderson. "Avoid Fort Bragg," the note said, "it ain't going to be healthy for you."[32]

By the time of Maxwell's success with *The Eve of St. Mark*, Hargrove, who after the war wrote the screenplay for the successful film *The Music Man* and wrote scripts for such television programs as *I Spy, Maverick*, and *The Waltons*, had joined the staff of *Yank*, the newly created army magazine run by enlisted men. According to Hargrove, Hartzell Spence, *Yank*'s executive editor, had seen a *PM* newspaper feature article with quotes from Hargrove's book. Spence plucked Hargrove from Fort Bragg's public relations office for the staff at the new weekly magazine, which opened its headquarters in May 1942 at 205 East Forty-second Street in New York under the direction of the Army Information and Education Division of the War Department's Army Service Forces.[33] Unlike the army newspaper *Stars and Stripes*, which had been established in World War I and

"HIS ORDERS CAME THROUGH JUST AS I [HARGROVE] WAS LEAVING AND [HE] LOOKED AS IF HE HAD JUST BECOME THE FATHER OF TRIPLETS." OVER THE BUS'S ENGINE HARGROVE COULD HEAR BUSHEMI CRY: "I'M GOING [TO YANK], I'M GOING, I'LL BE THERE NEXT WEEK.

YANK CORRESPONDENT MERLE MILLER AND BUSHEMI TAKE A SMOKE BREAK WHILE COVERING A TRAINING EXERCISE IN HAWAII WHERE THE TWO MEN HELPED INAUGURATE YANK'S PACIFIC EDITION.

MARY ELLEN CESSNA

overseen by officers, *Yank* had been created as a periodical managed by and devoted to the average enlisted man. Officers served only in an administrative function at *Yank*, which operated on a day-to-day basis just as a regular newsroom in civilian life. Joe McCarthy, the magazine's managing editor, noted that the two armed service publications worked together in harmony overseas because they were so different editorially. "*Yank* doesn't want the kind of news copy a *Stars and Stripes* editor demands and the *Stars and Stripes* isn't interested in *Yank*'s type of lengthy illustrated magazine article," said McCarthy.[34]

In an editorial in its first issue, *Yank* stated its aims: "Here's the YANK brother. This is our newspaper, solely and exclusively for us in the ranks and for nobody else. It's not G.I., except in the sense we are G.I. It's ours alone. . . . Because it is ours and because we are fighting men, it is here to reflect pride when we are proud, anger when we are sore. It is OUR record of what we're doing—in black and white." Priced at five cents a copy, *Yank* entertained the troops in its early days with such popular features as George Baker's "Sad Sack" cartoons; pin-ups of such Hollywood stars as Betty Grable, Rita Hayworth, Esther Williams, and Jane Russell; and a "Mail Call" where soldiers could air their gripes about life in the service. By the war's end, the magazine had 350 full-time staff members (plus an additional 1,000 stringers), published twenty-three separate editions, and had more than two million subscribers.[35]

When he learned about his close friend's departure for *Yank*, Bushemi, according to Hargrove, "fretted and cracked his knuckles for several days" before sending a scrapbook of his best pictures to *Yank*'s New York office. Bushemi had already attracted nationwide attention for his work, especially his photograph of an American

soldier posing on the crest of a hill; the image had appeared on the front cover of the January 1942 issue of the *Field Artillery Journal*. Impressed by Bushemi's photography skills, *Yank*'s editors invited him to join the staff. "His orders came through just as I was leaving," said Hargrove, "and Bushemi looked as if he had just become the father of triplets." He noted that he was about to leave Fort Bragg for New York on a bus with Shearer, who had also been tapped for a spot on *Yank*'s staff, when he spied his friend rushing toward him, waving and hollering. Over the bus's engine Hargrove could hear Bushemi cry: "I'm going [to *Yank*], I'm going, I'll be there next week."[36]

Bushemi became one of the first four photographers selected to join the *Yank* staff. In addition to Bushemi, the other cameramen for the magazine included Robert Ghio, a portrait photographer from Columbia, Missouri; Gordon T. Frye, an advertising and motion-picture still photographer from Newport and Providence, Rhode Island; and George Aarons, a photographer in the army's public relations office at West Point originally from Nashua, New Hampshire. According to one magazine article, the chief attribute that won the men spots on *Yank* was "sheer nerve, army brass."[37] Bushemi proved his worth just in time for the magazine's first issue, which was published on June 17, 1942. Bushemi played a key role, in fact,

in saving the fledgling publication from potential embarrassment. For its inaugural issue, *Yank* had focused on Congress's decision to increase monthly pay for soldiers and sailors. Sergeant Bill Richardson, the magazine's editor, had decided to highlight this decision, which raised a private's pay from $21 a month to $50 a month, by using on the cover a full-page photograph of a grinning GI holding a fistful of dollars with a headline announcing the wage hike. At the last minute, the magazine received a letter from President Franklin D. Roosevelt titled "Why We Fight." Hastily attempting to place the letter in the magazine in time for its publication, the editor placed on the cover a large headline, "F.D.R.: Why We Fight," above the illustration of the smiling soldier with the handful of cash. "The negative propaganda potential of this combination could have been disastrous—and would have lead to the immediate demise of *Yank*," said Art Weithas, the magazine's art editor. Approximately 50,000 copies of the issue had been printed before anyone noticed the awkward juxtaposition of the headline and photograph. The editors scrambled to find a replacement photograph, and found one—an image of an artillery battery in action taken by Bushemi.[38]

Over the next few months, Bushemi worked as a photographer for the magazine's New York

NOT ALL OF BUSHEMI'S ASSIGNMENTS IN THE PACIFIC INVOLVED THE GRITTY REALITY OF COMBAT. HERE, HE RELAXES WITH AN UNIDENTIFIED BATHING BEAUTY, PROBABLY A POTENTIAL SUBJECT FOR ONE OF *YANK*'S POPULAR PIN-UP PHOTOGRAPHS THAT ADORNED BARRACK-ROOM WALLS AROUND THE WORLD.

MARY ELLEN CESSNA

office, producing illustrations for articles on such subjects as women workers at Maryland's Aberdeen Proving Ground, army desert warfare maneuvers in California, and Corporal Robert Francis Mitchell's successful attempt to win a commission as a second lieutenant at Officer Candidate School at Fort Benning, Georgia. Bushemi seemed particularly pleased with his photographs for the Mitchell article, "Benning School for Boys," which was written by *Yank* staff member Walter Bernstein. "Ought to be damned good; it is coming out in next week's issue with five pages of space," Bushemi wrote his sister Mary Ellen. "Incidentally, my last assignments have been quite interesting. I returned and covered the last game of the World Series. Another job was to mug [actress] Madel[e]ine Carroll. As yet there are no future out-of-town assignments."[39]

Bushemi's excellent work for the magazine buttressed Spence's belief that it was essential to have photographers on *Yank*'s staff instead of relying upon the work of U.S. Army Signal Corps cameramen. In a memo to then Major Franklin S. Forsberg, *Yank*'s commanding officer, Spence said the magazine's approach to pictures was exclusively its own. Because the magazine took as long as two to eight weeks to reach its intended audience, it could not rely on Signal Corps photographs that would already have been published in daily and weekly

newspapers and magazines of large circulation. "The fundamental principle of YANK is that it is an enlisted men's paper," Spence added. "As much of the work as possible is directed to be done by enlisted men, from their point of view. Since a picture is worth a thousand words, this point of view must also be reflected in our pictures, and must be attuned to our editorial policy." Although *Yank* had established a good working relationship with the Signal Corps, which had cooperated with the magazine "to a degree beyond our hopes," Spence pointed out that Forsberg should not overlook the moral factor involved with having noncommissioned photographers taking pictures of enlisted men in action. "Our photographs," he said, "are the pictorial eye of all our enlisted men, and they are exceedingly proud of that fact, as they are proud of their own newspaper."[40]

In November 1942, Bushemi, joined by Miller, also an Iowa native and a former Washington correspondent for the *Philadelphia Record*, left New York for Hawaii to open *Yank*'s Pacific bureau. Traveling to Honolulu aboard the *SS Noordam*, a passenger liner from the Holland American Line converted for use by the navy as a troopship, Bushemi became enthralled by the beautiful sunsets he witnessed as the ship plied the waters of the Pacific Ocean. He observed that the sunsets reflected "thousands of colors on the water. And the waves that crashed against the sides, making bright reflections that overturned and disappeared." Bushemi also witnessed an albatross faithfully following the *Noordam*, something he said was "always thrilling to watch."

To pass the time on the long voyage, Bushemi did the usual amount of griping about the crowded conditions and cursing the poor quality of the food onboard. "We batted the breeze until our conversation ran out," he said. "We read books and magazines twice over." As soon as they had boarded the liner, Bushemi and Miller had been elected by their shipmates to publish a daily mimeographed newspaper. It was sometimes a hazardous operation; navy officers threatened to throw Miller into the brig after his front-page article featured a military map.[41]

The city of Honolulu had changed dramatically since Japan's surprise attack on Pearl Harbor. Bushemi said that its streets were jammed with soldiers, sailors, and civilians aiding the war effort. "In what used to be the 'Paradise of the Pacific' we have established fortifications and our citizens there are well-trained soldiers," he reported to the folks back home in Gary. "The islands have forever changed." The navy had taken over the luxurious Royal Hawaiian Hotel, where during peacetime a tourist had to pay $50 a day. People could still swim at Waikiki beach during daylight hours, Bushemi said, but swimmers had to sidestep the many barbed

wire emplacements. "It's the smell of gunfire now instead of the pikake flower," he said, adding that at night, the city became deserted with only a few civilian vehicles traveling on Honolulu's streets.[42]

After enduring a three-and-a-half-day quarantine, Miller and Bushemi established their living quarters at the Moana Seaside Bungalows in Waikiki and began the lengthy process of introducing themselves to army and navy officials. Writing Spence back in New York, Miller reported that working conditions with the army "will, I believe, be excellent. We will be extended all the rights and privileges of civilian correspondents— no more, no less." He also expressed the belief that *Yank* would prove to be popular with soldiers. While Miller and Bushemi were in quarantine, they noticed a pile of eight hundred copies of *Yank* were sold within five hours of being placed on sale.[43] Both Bushemi and Miller were eager to report on the American war against the Japanese, but instead they spent many quiet months in Honolulu covering training stories, searching for qualified soldiers to join *Yank*'s Hawaii office, struggling to circulate the magazine to its far-flung readership, and dealing with intransigent navy officials. The tedium was broken a bit for Bushemi when he received instruction in motion picture filming from Colonel Frank Capra, the famed Hollywood director. Bushemi later shot and edited

THE STAFF OF *YANK'S* PACIFIC EDITION GATHER AROUND COMMAND OFFICER CAPTAIN CHARLES W. BALTHROPE (THIRD FROM LEFT). THE STAFF INCLUDED (FROM LEFT TO RIGHT): MACK MORRISS, MERLE MILLER, BALTHROPE, UNIDENTIFIED WOMAN, BUSHEMI, AND LARRY MCMANUS.

MARY ELLEN CESSNA

his own movies, each of which began with the words "A One-Shot Production." The *Yank* duo did manage to produce an article on a Hawaiian pack train that used mules to carry ammunition, guns, and supplies up Oahu's mountains, fortified by the army to aid in halting any Japanese invasion. The men in the unit, Bushemi noted, were recruited from Texas cavalry units and were "tough as hell." Other feature articles the team produced for the magazine included a report on the only all-black combat unit stationed in Hawaii, known as "Hooper's Troopers" after their commanding officer, Colonel Chauncey M. Hooper, and a report on the Signal Corps's pigeon section, trained to use the birds to send distress messages. Joined by eighteen other soldiers (including infantry and artillery officers, sailors, and a handful of Pacific Rangers), Bushemi and Miller also participated in and reported on a jungle survival class taught by Dr. Kenneth P. Emory, an ethnologist at Honolulu's Bishop Museum.[44]

Writing Hargrove in December 1942 to congratulate him on his upcoming marriage, Bushemi said that although Hargrove's wife-to-be Alison might not like the idea, he inquired whether Hargrove and Shearer might be able to join him in Honolulu and work together in covering the Pacific theater. (Hargrove eventually reported on the action in China for *Yank*, while Shearer trans-

ferred to Armed Forces Radio.) "Between us gals," wrote Bushemi, "Forsberg [*Yank*'s commanding officer] has inquired about ficilities [*sic*] for printing the magazine here. It seems that this is the only thing left to do, as YANK is having difficulties aplenty with circulation." Bushemi added that he and Miller had been "working our fingers to the bone gathering news and picture material, and attempting some method of circulation. Its [*sic*] caused a roit [*sic*] of confusion." In addition to his busy schedule, Bushemi reported to his friend about the positive reception in Hawaii to Hargrove's book, *See Here, Private Hargrove*, which was "going over great guns." In fact, the last shipment of the book arriving via convoy was practically gone, he said, adding that he noticed a woman reading it on a bus, "constantly chuckling as she turned the pages."[45]

A particularly low moment for Bushemi and Miller came when Spence sent a note asking them to inject more warfare flavor into their articles along the lines of the reporting by *Yank* correspondent Mack Morriss about the pitched battle raging on Guadalcanal in the Solomon Islands. Although Spence said he was "highly pleased" with their work, he would continue to "hammer on the fact that your copy is too wordy and is not yet factual enough. Look at the stories Mack Morriss is writing from Guadalcanal and you will see what I mean about stories being factual. You can smell the Japs in his stories. That is what I mean by good reporting." Miller and Bushemi soon had an answer for the home office, reminding those back in New York: "This is not a combat zone. The only Japs you can smell here are the ones that ride beside you in Honolulu busses and street cars."[46]

Using Hawaii as their base, Miller and Bushemi did travel extensively on assignment for *Yank* to such locales as New Caledonia, the Fiji Islands, and Australia. "I guess we covered all of 52,000 miles on those trips," Miller later told a reporter.[47] The *Yank* correspondent marveled at his partner's ability to make friends with everyone from enlisted men to generals. It was not unusual, observed Miller, to see navy captains and army colonels and majors lugging Bushemi's camera cases and equipment around and driving him to wherever his assignment took him.[48] Writing to his brother, Frank, about his experiences with Miller, Bushemi reported: "Maybe by this time you know that we've been far in the south Pacific—Fiji, and New Caledonia. The places are rugged as hell. I would be very unhappy if I was assigned there. But, goddammit, we've got a good Army down to wonderful fighters." Bushemi also told his brother that to enliven a particularly slow week, he had composed a photograph about a new regulation ordering GIs to salute army nurses. "The Pix: A G.I.

throwing a high-ball (salute in Army language) to a luscious nurse in khaki," Bushemi wrote. "She returns the salute with her eyes and eye-brows cocked to one side and high into her forehead, sorta unexpected expression, as she puckered her high, thick, lovely, come-on lips. I captioned the shot: STRICTLY G-EYE. You have a good sense of humor, old man, [I] think you'll like it. If the pix ain't good, it's a good idea, anyway."[49]

During their travels, Miller and Bushemi were happy to discover that *Yank* had earned a solid reputation with American fighting men in the Pacific. "We aren't perfect yet—not by a long shot," Miller wrote the magazine's New York office, "but, so everyone tells us, we are getting better and better. The soldier likes us; the sailor likes us; the Marine likes us."[50] Even the army's public relations officers in the South Pacific developed a soft spot for the *Yank* staff members. Captain Reginald S. Jackson said his introduction to correspondents from *Yank* had always been via what he called the "barracks bag method," with an overloaded soldier dropping his bulging bag only to ask when and where food might be available. When Miller and Bushemi arrived at Jackson's office in Fiji, Miller introduced his photographer friend as a person "mentioned prominently" in Hargrove's *See Here, Private Hargrove*. While in Fiji, the two men "lived in style," according to

Jackson. They had met Dick Asquith of the Red Cross and managed to find bunks in Red Cross quarters located in a comfortable house off of the beaten track. "Bushemi had fallen afoul of our photographic officer by keeping the lab held up late one night," said Jackson, "so to patch matters up John, before he left, introduced the officer to a girl he had met . . . and according to last reports everyone concerned is living happily ever after."[51]

The happy-go-lucky tone of Jackson's recollection masked some deep frustrations felt by both Miller and Bushemi, particularly problems with moody officers and military censors. In one letter to *Yank*'s headquarters in May 1943, Miller noted that during the past month he and Bushemi had been working on a story involving hand-to-hand combat training being taught by Colonel Francois D'Eliscu. Unfortunately, on their fifth afternoon with D'Eliscu "his French temperament and John's Italian one came into conflict—and the fault was certainly not John's." It seemed that the colonel had his own ideas about what pictures should and should not be taken, and he refused to allow any of Bushemi's work to be released. When the *Yank* duo tried a second time to report on the story, they discovered a more helpful D'Eliscu. "Nevertheless," Miller pointed out, "we wasted five entire days so far as copy- and picture-getting are concerned." Just a week later, he and Bushemi

spent three days and three nights covering amphibious training exercises only to discover their work had been for naught. "Although we had been given the go-ahead by the censors—both Army and Navy, not a picture, not a line will be allowed," said Miller, who added that he and Bushemi possessed the faculty "for deciding what is restricted is just the thing for YANK—and this is probably the most restricted place in the world." The main problem with censorship often came from the navy, whose officers were unwilling to assist a couple of enlisted men and even suspected the *Yank* correspondent and photographer "of being saboteurs of some kind," Miller said.[52]

Matters began to improve for *Yank*'s Hawaii bureau with the arrival in June 1943 of Captain Charles W. Balthrope as commanding officer for the magazine's Pacific edition. Morriss, who had returned to Hawaii along with *Yank* combat artist Howard Brodie after covering the bitter fighting on Guadalcanal (Brodie returned to New York with a serious case of hepatitis while Morriss remained in Hawaii with Miller and Bushemi), said of Balthrope: "The captain made a terrific impression on us—he has one of the most forceful, and likable, personalities I've ever encountered. We hadn't known him an hour before we felt we were old buddies. He's that kind of guy."[53] Miller, too,

BUSHEMI TURNED IN TO YANK "EXCELLENT STUDIES OF JUNGLE OPERATIONS AND PORTRAITS OF THE BEARDED INFANTRYMEN WHO HAD SWEATED OUT THE BATTLES OF THE MUNDA AIRSTRIP AND HASTINGS RIDGE."

SERGEANT ARCHIE MCLEAN OF RHODES, MICHIGAN, PEERS FROM THE COVER OF YANK—ONE OF THE IMAGES BUSHEMI TOOK FOR A MORRISS ARTICLE ON INFANTRY BATTLES ON NEW GEORGIA. A VETERAN OF GUADALCANAL, MCLEAN AND HIS RIFLEMEN PROTECTED MACHINE-GUN CREWS ON NEW GEORGIA.

expressed his satisfaction with the new officer, writing Spence that both he and Bushemi were "delighted with the captain; we feel he is exactly the kind of Yank officer we hoped would be our representative out here."[54]

With an officer now on hand to deal with the myriad of difficulties facing *Yank*'s Hawaii office—everything from circulation to relations with local newspapers—Miller and Bushemi turned their attention to lobbying the magazine's New York office for a chance to report on combat operations in the Pacific, as both of them wanted to "see, picture and write some action," said Miller.[55] In August 1943 Bushemi finally had his chance to photograph combat, teaming with Morriss to cover the action on New Georgia, located northwest of Guadalcanal in the Solomon Islands. Acting on their own and without direct permission from *Yank*'s New York office, Bushemi and Morriss arrived at Munda, New Georgia, on August 15 after American forces had captured Munda Airfield but were still fighting the Japanese at Bairoko Harbor and Arundel Island.[56] Hargrove said his friend Bushemi turned in to *Yank* "excellent studies of jungle operations and portraits of the bearded infantrymen who had sweated out the battles of the Munda airstrip and Hastings Ridge." On these trips Bushemi was armed with his Bell and Howell movie camera, a Rolleiflex, and a Speed Graphic. The handheld Speed Graphic, which produced a four-inch by five-inch negative, was weighty and bulky, but it offered photographers distinct advantages in pursuing their craft, including interchangeable lenses, the choice of two shutters, and a film pack. "He used the Speed-Graphic in combat more than any of the other *Yank* photographers," Hargrove noted, "who, as a rule, prefer a small camera at the front lines."[57]

BRITISH EDITION

YANK

THE ARMY ~~WEEKLY~~

3d OCT. 17
1943
VOL. 2, NO. 18

By the men .. for the
men in the service

VETERANS OF MUNDA
AND GUADALCANAL

The Story of an Infantry Battle in New Georgia

PAGE 3

BRITISH EDITION

YANK

THE ARMY ⬤ WEEKLY

3 d NOV. 28
1943
VOL. 2, NO. 24
By the men .. for the
men in the service

THE ENEMY IS
VERY NEAR

Pictures of Clean-Up Operations in South Pacific

For American GIs and marines fighting in the Pacific, the terrain and climate proved to be almost as big of an obstacle as their Japanese opponents. Heavy monsoon rains on Cape Gloucester loosened the earth and caused huge trees to fall on advancing marines, killing dozens; bulldozers sank into the swampy ground on Bougainville; a group of engineers sent to survey the Santa Cruz Islands were felled not by bullets, but by cerebral malaria; and marines fighting desperately for survival on Peleliu had to endure temperatures that reached 115 degrees Fahrenheit in the shade. One corporal may have been speaking for many of those who endured battles in the Pacific when, told by a sergeant about the numerous obstacles facing the upcoming invasion of Saipan—dense jungle, quicksand, poisonous snakes, crocodiles, and sharks—the soldier asked: "Sarge, why don't we just let the Japs keep it?"[58]

Correspondents and photographers, too, had to battle the elements to reach the frontlines to gather material for their stories and photographs. Arriving on New Georgia in the Solomon Islands in mid-August 1943, Morriss and Bushemi embarked on an arduous journey to visit the 161st Infantry Regiment, which was camped on the crest of Mount Tiarakiamba after a successful operation to take Bairoko Harbor. The two men set out on foot in rainy weather "having no idea where it [Bairoko Harbor] was, how long it would take us, or anything else," said Morriss. For five hours the *Yank* correspondent and photographer struggled through a jungle so thick that for a time in the mid-afternoon it became too dark for the men to see clearly. "At first we walked fairly steadily," Morriss said, "but then took breaks faster and faster until we were resting almost every ten minutes; the mud when we started had a suction effect on our feet and then with the rain became slippery, clodding [*sic*] our shoes." The journey was

CORRESPONDENTS AND PHOTOGRAPHERS, TOO, HAD TO BATTLE THE ELEMENTS TO REACH THE FRONTLINES TO GATHER MATERIAL FOR THEIR STORIES AND PHOTOGRAPHS.

BUSHEMI CAPTURES THE TENSENESS OF COMBAT IN THE PACIFIC THEATER WITH HIS PHOTOGRAPH OF SOLDIERS WADING ACROSS THE ARUNDEL RIVER IN NEW GEORGIA.

particularly hard on Bushemi, his companion noted, because the photographer had yet to become acclimated to the tropical climate. They arrived "fatigued to an extreme" at the regiment's command post, Morriss noted, with a newfound respect for the soldiers who had to endure such hardships "day in and day out, carrying equipment, and then go into action. I realize now as never before that this battle is one of endurance against the elements as much as against the enemy."[59]

The *Yank* duo presented an odd sight to the men in the field. Gary, Indiana, native Keith Crown Jr. was looking over a rain-dampened map in a command post on the crest of Mount Tiarakiamba when he noticed two newcomers approaching via a muddy trail that wound its way through the dense jungle. The men, he later remembered, had their pants rolled high above their knees in a vain attempt to keep them clean from the heavy, soaking mud that now covered their legs. Both soldiers were also dripping wet and weighted down with sodden musette bags. After conferring with an officer, the newcomers were led off to find a spot to spend the night. A short while later, the officer returned with one of the men and introduced him to Morriss, who, because the commanding officer proved to be too busy to talk with him, proceeded to squat by Crown and pepper him with questions about the recent campaign. "I gave him what

information I knew, illustrating with some sketches made during the campaign," said Crown. "Finally, we arrived at that point where one asks the other where he's from. When I said 'Gary, Indiana,' Mack jumped up excitedly. 'Well for Chri' sake,' he said, and ran off shouting: 'Johnny.'"[60]

Morriss soon returned with his companion—Bushemi. "Johnny's hair was black, it went in all directions and like all of ours was badly in need of a barber," said Crown. "His eyes were dark and good natured; when he grinned his teeth seemed unusually white because of his swarthy complexion." The two men's conversation soon turned to a subject dear to the hearts of many Hoosiers: basketball. Discovering that Bushemi had been a photographer for the *Post-Tribune*, Crown asked if he knew his father, Keith Crown Sr., a basketball coach for many years at Gary's Horace Mann High School.[61] Bushemi did, and the two reminisced about the sport. Crown recalled that in some games a player would break away for a clear shot at the basket only to be blinded by the photographer's flash.

The rest of the day Morriss and Bushemi ferreted out information on possible photographs and articles on Crown's regiment and its part in the battle for the Munda Airfield. Later that night the trio, joined by Captain "Bobo" Berger, shared a meal together. It consisted of tea boiled in a number ten peach can, handfuls of rice from a Japanese supply dump, a can of GI hash, and a small can of pork loaf, "all mixed with rain water and heated in a helmet," said Crown. Crown noted that Bushemi called the dinner "one of the best meals he'd ever eaten—of course it was the first he'd eaten since some dog biscuits early that morning." Early the next day, Morriss and Bushemi left Crown to talk with members of the regiment's First Battalion.[62]

While working with Morriss covering fighting on Arundel and Sagekarsa Islands in the New Georgia group, Bushemi had his first experience of being under fire from the Japanese. Both men had vivid—if slightly different—impressions of the nighttime shelling. As the men dropped to the ground to avoid the shrapnel exploding near them, Morriss, wedged side-by-side with Bushemi in a narrow foxhole, noticed that the photographer was breathing "deeply and fast" and recognized for the first time in someone else a feeling he had experienced under fire from a sniper at Guadalcanal. "A feeling not so much fear, in fact not fear at all," said Morriss, "but the intense shock of realization that someone is trying in earnest to kill me. The shock is sudden, but it lingers not for long." Reading his friend's diary entry on the event, Bushemi had a different version. "Johnny noticed my breathing," Morriss noted, "and wondered if I had heart failure

or something because I was breathing deeply and fast, but I didn't notice myself but noticed Johnny, and Johnny didn't notice himself but noticed me, so that's the way it goes."[63] Writing to his sister Mary Ellen in Gary, Bushemi pointed out that it was not unusual for him to jump into a foxhole three or four times a night. "We were scared as hell when Jap artillery shelled us once, naturally we would be. I'll never forget that night because I was thinking of a million things at once."[64]

The appearance of a correspondent and photographer near the front lines drew plenty of "sarcastic humor" from the GIs, noted Morriss, who kidded Bushemi and some Signal Corps photographers accompanying them about snapping photos of the army instead of the usual shots of marines in action. Morriss quoted the soldiers' banter in his New Georgia diary as follows: "take my picture, buddy . . . hey boy right here put it in the paper back in the states joe blow on Arundel . . . been in these goddam jungles so long even the birds got friendly with us . . . what paper is this gonna be in fella . . . signal corps . . . i thought they was for life . . . you taking pictures for yank . . . christ what a racket . . . you in the army . . . hey boy take my picture." [65]

The partnership between Bushemi and Morriss proved to be a fruitful one for both men. They produced three features for *Yank*: "Story of an Infantry Battle in New Georgia," which appeared in the October 15, 1943, issue; "The Five-Day Attack on Hastings Ridge," which appeared on November 19, 1943; and "Jungle Mop-Up," which appeared on November 26, 1943. In detailing the photographs supplied to *Yank* by Bushemi, McCarthy, in a letter to Balthrope, praised both Morriss's writing and Bushemi's photography, particularly the "Story of an Infantry Battle in New Georgia" article. McCarthy said it was the first time the magazine had received "such a story with plenty of good pictures of people concerned to accompany it. Please tell Bushemi that we are very proud of the work he did on this trip to the South Pacific."[66] Unfortunately for the Morriss/Bushemi team, in the fall of 1943 Morriss received orders from *Yank* to return to its New York headquarters, and Bushemi had to return to Hawaii. (Morriss, an Elizabethton, Tennessee, native, went on to cover the fighting in Europe for *Yank*.)[67] "It made me mad as hell because we could've seen more action," Bushemi complained to McCarthy. "I want to see combat again and will try to swing a deal with Balthrope." Once back in Honolulu, Bushemi worked on the layout of the magazine's Hawaii edition and also selected photographs for the periodical as he waited for his next assignment, which was not long in coming.[68]

In November 1943 Admiral Raymond Spruance, in charge of the Fifth Fleet, headed Operation Galvanic in the central Pacific, whose objective was to seize two small atolls in the Gilbert Island chain: Tarawa and Makin. Bushemi participated in the invasion of Makin with the approximately 6,500 troops of the 165th Regimental Combat Team of the Twenty-seventh Infantry Division, a National Guard outfit from New York that had been on garrison duty in Hawaii. Although the initial landings on Makin met with little resistance from the estimated 800 Japanese forces (including a large number of Korean laborers) on the atoll, the inexperienced American forces made, according to marine General Holland "Howling Mad" Smith, "infuriatingly slow" progress and endured nighttime counterattacks and harassment by their foes. Hidden in trees, snipers threw firecrackers whose sound mimicked Japanese rifle fire. The corresponding response from GIs gave away their position to the enemy. As dawn approached, one Japanese solider went as far as to call out, "Reveille, fellows! Get up! Reveille!"[69]

Bushemi waded ashore on Makin with John Beaufort, a correspondent with the *Christian Science Monitor*. As his landing boat drove for shore, Bushemi spied his first enemy troops—two Japanese soldiers on a sampan that he fired at with

**MORRISS AND BUSHEMI TAKE A BREATHER WHILE COVERING COMBAT OPERATIONS
IN THE RUGGED JUNGLES OF NEW GEORGIA FOR** *YANK.*

LIBRARY OF CONGRESS, LC-USZ62-071766

his carbine. "I knew they were out of range," he said in a letter to Morriss, "but I fired anyway because I wanted that satisfaction." As Bushemi and Beaufort reached land, they looked up to see an American plane dive-bombing a Japanese 90-mm dual-purpose gun. "The Japs got the plane," Bushemi told Morriss, "and we could see three pieces disappear in the black smoke from an oil dump." Unlike the jungle fighting on New Georgia, Bushemi reported that the battle on Makin was a "dugout to dugout" affair. The photographer expressed admiration for the GIs mechanical ingenuity, noting that they could make anything run, including captured Japanese motorcycles and trucks.[70]

On his first night on Makin, Bushemi believed his foxhole to be "the worst in the world." He had to endure not only constant machine gun and sniper fire, but also a pesky creature: mosquitoes. "No one slept," he said, including his foxhole mate, Beaufort, who kept poking Bushemi all night to report sounds of movement around the area. "I had a carbine," wrote the photographer, "and would have shot at the least sound. It was a miserable night, and I'm glad it's over." As daylight operations closed on November 22, the remaining Japanese, fueled by alcohol, conducted what Bushemi termed "a wild and suicidal attack" that later earned the nickname "Sake Night." The fighting at times turned hand-to-hand, and the photog-

rapher reported that in the darkness one GI felt a Japanese soldier squeeze his ankle to discover whether he was dead or alive. "That was the Jap's last act, for the soldier finished him off with the butt of his rifle," said Bushemi. When daylight broke, three Americans lay dead and twenty-five wounded, while fifty-one enemy corpses lay on the battlefield. Finally, on November 23, General Ralph Smith signaled to Admiral Richmond Kelly Turner: "Makin taken."[71]

Although frightening, the Japanese response to the Makin operation resulted in slight U.S. ground casualties. The same could not be said for Tarawa, where the U.S. Marines were waging a bloody and desperate battle for survival that in the end claimed the lives of approximately 1,000 Americans and 4,700 Japanese. The ferocity of the fighting, and photographs of American dead littering the beaches, shocked a complacent American public that had "never been led to expect anything but an easy war," noted *Time* correspondent Robert Sherrod.[72] While at Makin, Bushemi heard about the tremendous fighting still going on at Tarawa, tossed his exposed negatives to McManus for later development in Hawaii, and then convinced Lieutenant Colonel James Roosevelt to fly him to Tarawa aboard a seaplane. "It was characteristic of Johnny that he went into the thick of it at Tarawa under no compulsion whatever," said Miller, who dedicated his 1945 World War II novel, *Island 49*, to his friend. "It was never required of him to go out into actual combat, but he never missed a chance to go. He felt it was part of his job to be where the fighting was."[73]

When Bushemi finally reached Tarawa he was surprised at how small and flat it appeared from the air. As his plane flew over the atoll, he saw hundreds of bodies with their equipment gone floating in the water—all of them dead American marines. "The courage of our marines was magnificent," Bushemi later wrote, "and it made me proud that my brother, Sam, is a member of the corps."[74] The fighting on the island had ended, but Bushemi did manage to witness some of the mopping-up operation of the last Japanese who refused to surrender. Writing Morriss, Bushemi described Tarawa as being similar in appearance to the landscape the two men had experienced on Munda in New Georgia with an airstrip and reinforced pillboxes for defense. "But that first day on Tarawa I saw the most fantastic sights I've ever seen, those Marines on the beaches," admitted Bushemi.[75]

His presence at the scene of one of the war's bloodiest battlefields gave Bushemi the opportunity to take on another assignment for *Yank*—that of writer. The magazine's December 24, 1943, issue featured his article "Death Battle at Tarawa." In the piece, which received extensive editorial revision from *Yank*'s editors in New York, he described the Second Marine Division's determined assault of the heavily defended atoll:

Even the dead Marines were determined to reach Tarawa's shore.

As one Higgins landing boat roared toward the dry sand, you could see a hand clutching its side. It was the hand of a Marine, frozen in the grip of death.

The Second Marine Division took this island because its men were willing to die. They kept on coming in the face of a heavy Jap defense, and though they paid the stiffest price in human life per square yard that was ever paid in the history of the Marine Corps, they won this main Jap base in the Gilbert Islands in 76 hours.

Out of two battalions—2,000 to 3,000 men—thrown onto the beach in the first assault at 0830, only a few hundred men escaped death or injury. Officer casualties were heavy. And still the Marines kept coming. The Leathernecks died with one thought—to get there.

Before dawn of the first day of the invasion, the Navy opened up with a tremendous bombardment. Carrier planes dropped 800 tons of bombs while battleships, cruisers, and destroyers hurled 2,000 tons of shells on an area two and a quarter miles long and at no point more than 800 yards wide. This was Beito, the fortified airstrip that is the main island of 26 comprising the Tarawa atoll.

The Marines were to hit the sandy beach immediately after these softening-up operations ceased, and everybody on the boats was happy because it seemed like very effective fire, the kind of intense blasting that would make the Japs "bomb happy." But that wasn't the way it worked out.

The Japs were too well dug in. Their blockhouses were of concrete five feet thick, with palm tree trunks 18 inches in diameter superimposed on the concrete. And superimposed on the trees were angle irons made of railroad steel. On top of these were 10 to 12 feet of sand and coral rock. Only a direct hit by a 2,000-pound bomb would cave in or destroy such blockhouses.

The Jap pillboxes were built out of sand-filled oil drums, buttressed by heavy coconut logs and then sandbags. Air-raid shelters were constructed from coconut tree trunks, piled high in two walls, with coral sand filling the space in between.

Our heavy machine guns and 75s couldn't penetrate these emplacements or knock out the enemy eight-inch shore batteries and machine guns that were awaiting our assault waves.[76]

Although Bushemi's photographs of the Makin operation received extensive play in *Yank*, including appearing on the cover of the magazine's December 31, 1943, edition and a number inside for McManus's article "Shamrocks at Makin," his pictures of the action on Tarawa were not published. In a letter to Bushemi, McCarthy noted that he had held the cover open for the Makin photographs, which had shown up at the office just in the knick of time. "I am sorry to say that your radio photos of the Tarawa pictures did not turn out so well," McCarthy said. The magazine would have gladly used the wire-photos if no other pictures had been available, but McCarthy said *Yank* had been able to obtain photographs of the invasion from marine photographers. "By the time our magazine gets out with a wire-photo from overseas," he said, "the newspapers have usually published originals of the same picture. That is why we are not keen on wire-photos, except in rare cases." McCarthy praised Bushemi for his presence of mind in getting to Tarawa and for his "swell job" overall.[77]

With the completion of the campaign in the Gilbert Islands, Bushemi began to understand for the first time his friend Morriss's feelings about his experiences in the Solomon Islands. Writing Morriss in early January 1944, Bushemi outlined for Morriss his experiences covering the operations in the Gilberts and told him how much he had enjoyed working with the veteran correspondent in New Georgia. Bushemi noted:

I will never forget the things we sweated out together, especially that night when "pistol pete" [a Japanese plane that bombed late at night] got pretty close, and that night on the LST [landing ship, tank] when the moon was bright. I was scared as hell because I was green and didn't know what to expect. And I want you to know, Mack, that now, after participating in an original operation like the Gilberts, I know exactly how you felt that day on Guadalcanal when we toured with Mrs. F.D.R. and you stood on hill and valley and talked to me about actions you saw. It was hard for me to realize then how a place could become civilized. And I know now how you felt because the same thing has happened to me. Going into Makin was quite an experience and I don't want to ever see Makin again because I don't want to feel the way you did that day. I got a certain satisfaction of participating in the

operation, that was fine. And I don't want to go back there because I will never recognize it.[78]

In spite of being the only photographer to cover both invasions, Bushemi expressed unhappiness about the quality of his work. Although Hargrove considered Bushemi's photographs of the Makin operation some of the finest ever to be published in *Yank*, Bushemi did not agree. Instead, he wrote to editor Leo Hofeller to credit him for the fine job he had done in laying out the photographs in the magazine. "They looked fine because you saved for me what was lousy photography," he wrote Hofeller. "I'll try hard next time to get you better pictures." Noting that he and Miller were shortly to travel on another mission, Bushemi vowed that unless his work improved, he would quit and come back home.[79] The editors at *Yank*'s New York offices, however, had nothing but praise for the photographer's efforts, particularly the 1,600 feet of motion picture film showing the action in the Gilberts. "All are in agreement that it is an exceedingly fine job and you are to be highly commended for your work on it," Forsberg, the officer in charge of *Yank*, wrote Bushemi. "The Film Section at Astoria, which is using the film in the composition of a documentary film on the taking of Makin, believes that your material is far superior to that gathered by [the] Signal Corps,

. . . THE PACIFIC CLIMATE
PROVED TO BE SO
DIFFICULT THAT CAMERAS
HAD TO BE CLEANED AND
OILED AFTER EVERY USE,
AND THE FUNGUS BUILDUP
ON LENSES WAS SO GREAT
THAT CAMERAMEN SPENT
CONSIDERABLE TIME
DISASSEMBLING THEIR
OPTICS TO KEEP
THEM CLEAR.

RELAXING IN MAKESHIFT QUARTERS
SOMEWHERE IN THE PACIFIC,
BUSHEMI TAKES TIME TO CLEAN
HIS EQUIPMENT, A ROUTINE MATTER
GIVEN THE HARSH CLIMATE. THE
BATTERED EQUIPMENT CASE ON
THE GROUND IS LABELED
"ONE SHOT BUSHEMI."
LIBRARY OF CONGRESS, LC-USZ62-17409

and state that it will form the largest part of their film on Makin." McCarthy added the strongest rejoinder to Bushemi's self-criticism, writing the photographer: "First of all, if you think you did a lousy job on the Gilbert Islands . . . you have rocks in your head. The pictures were not quite as good as the ones you did in New Georgia but surely that was no fault of yours. Considering the material that you had to work with, I think you did a very swell job and I think that the moving pictures you took were terrific." McCarthy added that there were several officers in the audience at the Astoria studios who had worked in Hollywood and if he told Bushemi of their comments "that little head of yours would swell up like a basketball. Seriously, John, you are doing okay and for Christ's sake don't get downhearted."[80]

Bushemi's frustration over his work may have been prompted by the difficult conditions facing photographers in the Pacific. The hot and humid weather prevalent on most islands played havoc with both cameras and film. In his history of combat photographers of World War II, Peter Maslowski pointed out that the Pacific climate proved to be so difficult that cameras had to be cleaned and oiled after every use, and the fungus buildup on lenses was so great that cameramen spent considerable time disassembling their optics to keep them clear. Those photographers covering amphibious operations also had to guard their equipment against the corrosive salt spray kicked up by the churning landing craft.[81] Finding the necessary parts to make repairs also proved to be a difficult task. On one visit to Guadalcanal with Morriss, Bushemi discovered that his camera had been broken during the trip. Luckily for his partner, Morriss noted, he was at the "only place within 1000 miles [that] could have done the job." During his visit to New Georgia with Morriss, Bushemi

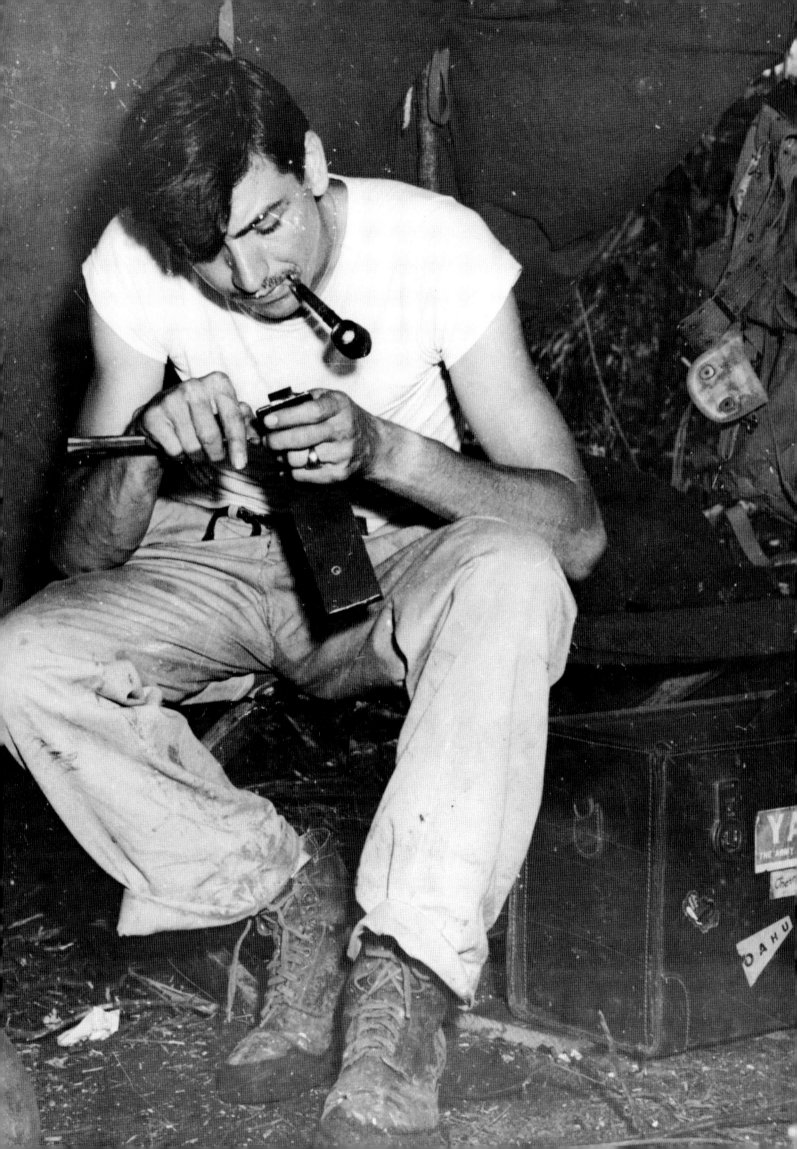

BUSHEMI AND SOME MARINES . . . RAIDED A DUGOUT AMPLY STOCKED WITH JAPANESE SAKE. ". . . TWO-HUNDRED GUYS LEFT THE M1S AND MACHINE-GUN POSITIONS FOR A DRINK."

BUSHEMI SMILES THROUGH THE PAIN OF AN INJURY HE SUFFERED TO HIS HAND WHILE COVERING THE INVASION OF THE KWAJALEIN ATOLL.
MARY ELLEN CESSNA

also had to use gun oil and then lighter fluid in order to clean his Speed Graphic's shutter-speed mechanism.[82]

For his next assignment, the invasion of Kwajalein atoll (the largest coral atoll in the world) in the Marshall Islands in late January 1944, Bushemi was reunited with Miller. While Miller covered the campaign—code-named Operation Flintlock—with the army's veteran Seventh Infantry Division as it attacked Kwajalein Island (home to the Japanese naval base) in the south, Bushemi worked with the untried Fourth Marine Division during its attack on Roi (location of the Japanese airfield) and Namur Islands in the north. "We figure for an overall coverage," Bushemi wrote McCarthy, "its [sic] best to be separated. I promise a good story because its [sic] going to be exciting for us."[83] Relying on improved tactics, firepower, and equipment, the American forces successfully captured the atoll—whose defenses were as formidable as those on Tarawa—at only a fraction of the cost in men and material.[84] In describing the battle to McCarthy, *Yank*'s managing editor, Bushemi was particularly impressed by the U.S. Navy's two-day pounding of the Japanese fortifications. "It was a very excellent job of softening up and when our Marines landed they met little resistance compared to Tarawa," he noted, adding there was little doubt among the troops that the bombardment had saved many lives. "Tarawa was a lesson to us because we learned about those strong blockhouses, but they [the Japanese] died in there." Noting that the Americans had no opposition from the air, Bushemi added that the scuttlebutt among the troops included a Japanese fleet sailing from its base at Truk to attack the invasion fleet. "They never showed up," he noted.[85]

On January 31, 1944, the marines quickly captured the lightly defended islets of Mellu and Ennubirr, which were then used by the

marines as bases for artillery attacks in support of the landings on Roi and Namur. The next day—despite what Bushemi called "a thick fog and rain"—the leathernecks moved on to the tougher task of capturing Roi and Namur (the two islands were joined together by an artificial causeway). Charles R. Vandergrift, a combat correspondent with the Fourth Marine Division, accompanied Bushemi on the landings at Mellu and Ennubirr, and at Roi and Namur, which proved to be "hot, so hot, in fact, that the beach and offensive front were synonymous," Vandergrift noted. A Navy ensign, commanding a small landing craft, dropped the two men on a pier. "You staying around awhile?" Vandergrift quoted Bushemi as asking the ensign. "Hell no!" the ensign shouted. "I'm getting out of here." The ensign ordered his coxswain to "rev up the motors, and away he went," said Vandergrift. "Johnny and I crouched behind a stack of perforated oil drums for a few minutes, decided there was [*sic*] no future stories, nor pictures here, and moved up to the beach."[86]

Although initially stunned by the heavy naval gunfire expended by the American fleet, the Japanese defenders displayed their usual tenacity during the invasion. Marines equipped with flamethrowers were thrown against the Japanese still alive in their pillboxes. "Many land mines exploded causing casualties, but the Marines kept

on driving," said Bushemi. "When Marines got close to Jap pillboxes the Japs exploded them. Or Japs would come out of their holes with their hands up holding a remote control and explode mines and pillboxes." With the island nearly secure, Bushemi and some marines he had befriended raided a dugout amply stocked with Japanese sake. "No kidding, two-hundred guys left the M1s and machine-gun positions for a drink. A Marine officer discovered that his men fled their front-line positions. It was the funniest thing you ever saw," Bushemi wrote McCarthy, "because he ran up to these guys and seized their bottles and started breaking them all around the place. The men just looked at him dumb-like and wouldn't leave the sake for a trip back to the states."[87]

While covering the action in the Marshall Islands (his photographs appeared in *Yank*'s March 10, 1944, issue along with Miller's article, "After the Battle at Kwajalein"), Bushemi suffered a hand injury. After gathering information for an article on the Seventh Infantry Division's reconnaissance troops, Miller and Bushemi were returning from a destroyer to their original transport onboard a landing craft in rough seas when a pulley rope broke loose, sending a davit crashing into Bushemi's left hand and fracturing a finger in the process. "When the finger had been splinted," said Miller, who had been hit in the head by the davit but escaped injury thanks to his helmet, "I tried to urge Johnny to go back to Honolulu, but he hardly listened to me. He knew another operation (Eniwetok) was coming up, and he wanted to go along."[88]

American planners had intended to attack Eniwetok atoll, located about 350 miles northwest of Kwajalein, in May, but the success of the previous operation caused them to launch the assault ahead of schedule. Although he had to operate his camera with one hand because of his injury, Bushemi refused to stay behind, traveling to the invasion with Miller aboard the *U.S.S. Neville*, a Heywood-class attack transport on which he had also sailed during the Makin operation. During those cruises Bushemi had made many friends on the ship. "We all liked him for his happy disposition and his willingness to share the discomforts of our crowded life, and the sacrifices it brought," noted Father James H. McConnell, a Catholic priest who served as the *Neville*'s chaplain. The ship's captain, Bradford Bartlett, and crew had been especially pleased with Bushemi's photographs of a "hilarious ceremony of crossing the equator," which made their way onto the pages of *Yank*.[89]

On February 19, 1944, Bushemi landed on Red Beach on Eniwetok Island with Miller and other correspondents during the fourth wave of troops. "From our troopships only a few hundred yards offshore, all of Eniwetok seemed to be on fire," reported Miller. "Red, yellow and black smoke blanketed the island, while a dull gray smoke clung to the shattered trees and bushes." During the landings of the first four waves, Miller said, there seemed to be little or no opposition from the Japanese defending the 4,700-yard-long, 250-yard-wide island. "The only sounds were from our own BAR [Browning automatic rifle] and rifle fire, spraying every tree that looked as if it might contain a sniper and every exposed shell crater," Miller told *Yank* readers. In fact, the correspondent heard one veteran of three previous assault landings comment: "This is the easiest one yet." Minutes later, however, the enemy responded to the attack with rifle fire and knee-mortar shells that fell among the GIs still on the beach. Enemy units hid in foxholes and spider trenches, firing on the Americans from behind as they advanced. "None of the holes was large enough to accommodate more than six Japs," wrote Miller, "and almost all of them were so well hidden that it was possible to step over and beyond the holes without seeing them. The Japs had allowed platoon after platoon of American troops to pass through before they opened up."[90]

Separated during the fighting, Bushemi and Miller, joined by correspondents from the *Chicago Tribune* and *Chicago Daily News* and photogra-

IN ADDITION TO SHOOTING STILL PHOTOGRAPHS, BUSHEMI EXPERIMENTED WITH TECHNICOLOR MOVIES, USING A BELL AND HOWELL MOVIE CAMERA. HE CUT AND EDITED THE RESULTING FOOTAGE HIMSELF AND EVEN WROTE HIS OWN SUBTITLES FOR THE ACTION ON THE SCREEN.

MARY ELLEN CESSNA

phers from other services, left the front for the beach early in the afternoon. Finding shelter behind an American medium tank, the men stopped to compare notes and smoke cigarettes. After witnessing a strafing run by Gruman Avenger aircraft, the group had gone ahead to survey the damage, with Bushemi, winding his movie camera, a few yards behind when the others stopped to examine a bullet-riddled chest filled with Marshellese books. As Miller stayed behind to pick up a Marshallese Bible, the rest of the men were moving forward when the first 60mm knee-mortar shells hit. "Each explosion kicked up dirt and sand as it landed; we thought each shell would be our last," said Miller. "No one knows how many bursts there were in all—probably five or six—but after two or three minutes the explosions stopped." During the lull in battle, Miller discovered that Captain Waldo Drake, a Pacific Fleet public relations officer, and Harold Smith, a correspondent for the *Chicago Tribune*, had both been wounded. Recalling the combat, Drake noted that a shell fragment hit the front lip of his helmet with so much force that it tossed him over backwards. Through the blood that spurted over his eyes, Drake could "see Bushemi try to rise and then fall back on the ground." Bushemi had been the most seriously wounded in the party, losing "tremendous amounts of blood" due to shrapnel

wounds in his left cheek, neck, and left leg. Miller and the others carried Bushemi about twenty feet and placed him in a shallow hole on the beach. While Hal O'Flaherty of the *Chicago Daily News* watched over his stricken comrade, Miller, Smith, and Drake (who refused treatment for his own wound) hurried about three hundred yards down the beach to an aid station.[91]

As Bushemi lay injured, Gus Mitchell of Richmond, Indiana, serving as a combat medic with the 106th Infantry, was pinned down on the beach by Japanese fire. Scanning ahead, Mitchell remembered seeing a figure appearing from the bush "wearing a GI helmet, khaki pants, and shirt. He had no weapons and was shouting for help. That someone was hurt." Joined by two litter bearers, Mitchell followed the soldier as sniper fire whined and mortars crashed all around the party. After a harrowing time—the medic remembered stumbling over the leg of a dead Japanese soldier—Mitchell finally reached the wounded American, who he learned was Bushemi. "I took a bandage and put pressure on the [head] wound," Mitchell noted. "All this was doing was soaking up the bandages with blood, so I took that off and put direct pressure [on the wound] with my fingers. This helped and I was able to stop the squirting of blood from the temple." Bushemi received sulfa and plasma injections and, as Mitchell continued

to put direct pressure on the head wound, the two litter bearers placed Bushemi on a stretcher and carried him—dodging the constant Japanese firing and shelling—to an aid station located about one hundred yards inland from where he had been hurt.[92] As he was being carried to the aid station, Bushemi, said Miller, asked about the condition of his cameras. "To reassure him," Miller said, "we put the cameras on the litter where he could keep his eyes on them."[93]

Moved again to an advanced aid station, Bushemi received another plasma injection and had his leg placed in a temporary cast. Before leaving the island for a navy transport, Bushemi joked with Miller, asking him "about the chances of his getting a plane back to Honolulu, and how long I thought he'd be hospitalized." The photographer also inquired about Drake's condition. After being placed on a landing boat, the wounded Bushemi was taken back to the *Neville* and immediately admitted to the ship's sick bay. "The navy doctors had to give him ether so they could tie some severed arteries which had caused him such serious blood loss from his neck wound," said Miller, "and it was after the anesthetic was administered that Johnny passed away—about 5:50 p.m. His last words to me, before he went to sleep, were: 'Be sure to get those pictures back to the office.'"[94]

On February 22 the navy held a memorial service onboard the *Neville* for Bushemi and an officer from the ship also killed in the fighting. In a letter to the Bushemi family, McConnell, who conducted the service for the fallen men, noted that he had given their son "the last rites of the Church as soon as he was brought up [to the ship]." Reporting on the ceremony in *Yank*, Miller noted that "sailors in work-grimed dungarees, soldiers in fatigues with the stains of battles, and casualties in hospital whites crowded the quarter deck as two flag-draped bodies were carried from the sick bay." One of the bodies was

"SO MANY PEOPLE BELIEVE, ALONG WITH ME, THAT A MAN WITH SUCH WARMTH AND ENERGY CAN'T POSSIBLY BE GONE, JOHN HAD MANY FRIENDS, I KNEW THAT, BUT I CERTAINLY DIDN'T REALIZE THERE WERE THOUSANDS. I REALLY BELIEVE HE WAS AS WELL KNOWN AND WELL LIKED AS ANYONE IN THIS ENTIRE THEATRE."

FATHER JAMES H. MCCONNELL LEADS THE MEMORIAL SERVICE FOR BUSHEMI AND KERMIT CHAPMAN ONBOARD THE *U.S.S. NEVILLE*. REPORTING ON THE PHOTOGRAPHER'S DEATH, *TIME* MAGAZINE CALLED BUSHEMI "PROBABLY THE BEST KNOWN NONCOM IN THE PACIFIC AREA."
MARY ELLEN CESSNA

Bushemi, while the other was Lieutenant Kermit Chapman of Fargo, North Dakota. Miraculously, to Miller, the sounds of battle faded as a nearby destroyer stopped its firing and Navy Avengers flying overhead were too high to be heard. Captain Bartlett came down from the bridge to start the service and an honor guard of seamen "brought their rifles to 'present arms,'" said Miller, and the ship's officers gathered around their fallen comrades. After McConnell read the Catholic committal service, the ship's colors were lowered to half-mast and a bugler blew attention as first sailors lowered Bushemi's body over the side to a waiting assault craft, followed by Chapman's remains. Bartlett ordered the craft to shove off and carry out its orders. Miller noted that the "sound of taps drifted out over the blue-white water" as the boat "headed northeast toward tiny, green and peaceful Japtan Island, unscarred by battle."[95] News of Bushemi's death did not reach Gary, however, until February 29 when his family received a telegram reading: "The secretary of war desires me to express his deep regret that your son, technician 3rd grade John A. Bushemi, was killed in action in defense of his country on Feb. 19 in Eniwetok atoll, Marshall Group. Letter follows."[96]

His fellow *Yank* correspondents overseas learned about Bushemi's fatal wounding in a March 2, 1944, letter from McCarthy. After sharing Miller's cabled story on the photographer's death, and praising him as a "swell sincere hard-working kid," McCarthy predicted that Bushemi "would have done big things in photography after the war if he had lived." Although Bushemi did not know it at the time, he had been scheduled to return to the states after his assignment in the Marshall Islands, said McCarthy. "We'll never be able to replace him," he said. Still, McCarthy told the overseas correspondents that the magazine planned no "fuss" over Bushemi's death in *Yank*'s pages "because, after all, death is a routine thing in the Army and we must continue to treat it as such when it hits one of our own men." To do otherwise, he added, would make the magazine look like "a Boy Scout publication."[97]

Miller, who had accompanied Bushemi on many operations in the Pacific and stayed by his side until the end, took the Hoosier's death very hard. Miller admitted to *Yank* artist Robert Greenhalgh that for awhile he had been "pretty well knocked out, but I now feel, as I know John felt, that all of us on YANK are soldiers, taking our chances on operations like the rest."[98] In a subsequent letter to Morriss, Miller noted he had been going through Bushemi's personal belongings in an attempt to get them in order for return to his family in Gary. "Honolulu seems vastly different now," said Miller. "So many people believe, along with me, that a man with such warmth and energy can't

A WHITE-HAIRED PIETRO BUSCEMI (CENTER OF PHOTOGRAPH WITH HIS BACK TO THE CAMERA) LOOKS ON AS HIS SON'S CASKET IS CARRIED INTO SAINT MARK CATHOLIC CHURCH IN GARY, INDIANA, IN NOVEMBER 1947.

MARY ELLEN CESSNA

possibly be gone, John had many friends, I knew that, but I certainly didn't realize there were thousands. I really believe he was as well known and well liked as anyone in this entire theater." Miller went on to say that he was working to obtain a posthumous Silver Star for Bushemi and had also suggested to McCarthy in New York the possibility of naming a Liberty Ship after the photographer. (Bushemi eventually received a Bronze Star in recognition of his achievements.)[99]

Bushemi's friends and associates expressed their grief over the loss of their friend in solemn letters to the photographer's family. Writing to Mary Ellen, Hargrove noted that he had looked on Bushemi "more as a brother than as a friend." Hargrove and his wife, Alison, were busy making plans for a welcome home party for Bushemi in New York when they heard about his fatal wounding. The photographer's death in battle seemed to Hargrove to be "one of the strangest and most incongruous commentaries on all of war; he was a man of peace, a man in whom I saw no malice or ill will toward anyone in all the time I knew him."[100] Lloyd Shearer, who served with Bushemi at Fort Bragg, wrote from his post at the Armed Forces Radio Service that when he heard the news of the photographer's death "it was as if a dagger had been thrust hilt-deep into my heart."[101] In a letter to Bushemi's father and stepmother

(Pietro Buscemi had married Carmella Leonardo in 1940), Morriss admitted there was little he could say to offer comfort to the family. Bushemi's friends, wrote Morriss, heard of his death first with disbelief and then with "great sorrow," as the photographer was someone "we all liked and respected and admired not only as a newspaper man but as a person." Morriss went on to note:

I have said this inadequately. Johnny was much more than that. I have known him since the beginning here at Yank. We went cross-country together en route to San Francisco and eventually were re-united in Honolulu last summer. It was when he and I went south to cover the New Georgia campaign in the Solomons that I really learned to know Johnny. He was one of my closest friends and, under fire, he was a man of real courage.

I am glad that Merle [Miller] was with him when he died. And I'm sure of one thing: that at the time he was hit, Johnny was doing the thing he wanted to do . . . taking pictures in the thick of the action.[102]

The letters of condolence from his colleagues on *Yank* cushioned the blow somewhat for the Bushemi family. Responding to Hargrove's expression of regret, Mary Ellen thanked him for his "very kind letter" and offered her own sympathy to her brother's longtime friend, noting: "Johnny was very fond of you, talked about you a great deal of the time, admired you not only as a marvelous writer but also admired you as a genuine companion." Her brother, she added, would always "live forever within me. I am proud of the work he has done for our country, I am proud of the way he died."[103]

Family and friends held a memorial service for Bushemi in Gary on March 3, 1944. Erwin Crewe Rosenau, a *Post-Tribune* reporter who covered the service, wrote that Bushemi would have "blushed furiously" over the laudatory comments made about him by Monsignor Joseph S. Ryder. "But his artistic soul," said Rosenau, "would have been delighted with the quiet beauty of the service, by the sight and sound of the children's choir in their white vestments." Those gathered at the service included Franz Allebach, former chief of the newspaper's photo department; H. B. Snyder, *Post-Tribune* editor in chief; and Elmer F. Budlove and Herbert Lukman, Bushemi's former colleagues on the newspaper's photography staff. Also on hand were representatives from the local draft board, Chicago newspapermen, and other *Post-Tribune* staff members. Fellow Gary veteran Sam Catanzarite, copilot of a B-24 bomber who had seen Bushemi in the Pacific and spent leaves with him in Hawaii, expressed no surprise about the

photographer's death. "I had a feeling that Johnny's number would come up one day," Catanzarite told Rosenau, "for he was always right up there at the frontline getting his pictures."[104]

In April 1944 the Gary Public Library's central branch at Fifth and Adams Streets hosted an exhibition of 200 of Bushemi's photographs, 150 of which were made available by *Yank*, with the others including his work at the *Post-Tribune* and images of the photographer in action. Sponsored by *Yank* and the *Post-Tribune*, the exhibition, which ran from April 30 to May 21, also included letters from high-ranking army officials praising Bushemi's career. That June, Lieutenant General Robert C. Richardson Jr., commander of U.S. forces in the Pacific theater, announced that the army had awarded Bushemi a Bronze Star. The citation for the award noted: "By his personal bravery, initiative and professional ability he produced photographs of such technical excellence and high quality that they attracted wide praise and admiration. The armed forces have gained materially by these candid portrayals of the fighting foot soldier. In order to accomplish his task he voluntarily chose the most dangerous phases of attacks. He thus obtained superior combat photographs."[105]

In October 1947 the ship *Honda Knot* sailed into San Francisco harbor carrying the flag-draped remains of three thousand American service-

NOTES

INTRODUCTION HOME FRONT, BATTLEFRONT, AND THE "GOOD WAR"

1. For good recent general studies of the home front, see Allan M. Winkler, *Home Front U.S.A.: America during World War II*, second edition (Wheeling, Ill.: Harlan Davidson, 2000); John W. Jeffries, *Wartime America: The World War II Home Front* (Chicago: I. R. Dee, 1996); Michael C. C. Adams, *The Best War Ever: America and World War II* (Baltimore: Johns Hopkins University Press, 1994). For Indiana during the war, see the special issue of *Traces of Indiana and Midwestern History* 3 (fall 1991); James H. Madison, *Indiana through Tradition and Change: A History of the Hoosier State and Its People, 1920-1945* (Indianapolis: Indiana Historical Society, 1982), 370-407; Max Parvin Cavnes, *The Hoosier Community at War* (Bloomington: Indiana University Press, 1961).

2. *Indiana Year Book*, 1942, p. 850.

3. George M. Blackburn, "The Hoosier Arsenal" (Ph.D. dissertation, Indiana University, Bloomington, 1956), 50-52, 218, 229-35, 224-80, 303-5, and 482.

4. Hugh M. Ayer, "Hoosier Labor in the Second World War" (Ph.D. dissertation, Indiana University, Bloomington, 1957), 357-61; Lynn W. Turner and Heber P. Walker, comps., *Indiana at War: A Directory of Hoosier Civilians Who Held Positions of Responsibility in Official, Volunteer and Cooperating War-Time Organizations* (Bloomington: Indiana War History Commission, 1951), 1056-57.

5. John Bartlow Martin, "Is Muncie Still Middletown?" *Harper's Magazine* 189 (July 1944): 98; Chad Berry, *Southern Migrants, Northern Exiles* (Urbana: University of Illinois Press, 2000), 82-101.

6. Cavnes, *The Hoosier Community at War*, 108-79; Emma Lou Thornbrough and Lana Ruegamer, *Indiana Blacks in the Twentieth Century* (Bloomington: Indiana University Press, 2000), 95-114; Harvard Sitkoff, "Willkie as Liberal: Civil Liberties & Civil Rights," in James H. Madison, ed., *Wendell Willkie: Hoosier Internationalist* (Bloomington: Indiana University Press, 1992), 71-87.

7. I. C. B. Dear, ed., *The Oxford Companion to World War II* (New York: Oxford University Press, 1995), 290.

8. Ayer, "Hoosier Labor in the Second World War," 236; Calvin C. Berlin, "Indiana's Civilian Soldiers" (Ph.D. dissertation, Indiana University, 1956), 129-36; *Indiana Year Book*, 1946, p. 668; Turner and Walker, *Indiana at War*, 557; John Bodnar, *Our Towns: Remembering Community in Indiana*

(Indianapolis: Indiana Historical Society, 2001), 67; James H. Madison, *Eli Lilly: A Life, 1885-1977* (Indianapolis: Indiana Historical Society, 1989), 78-79.

9. Berlin, "Indiana's Civilian Soldiers," 227; Marian McFadden, *Biography of a Town: Shelbyville, Indiana* (Shelbyville, Ind.: Tippecanoe Press, 1968), 315; John Paul Duncan, "Control of City Government in Indianapolis Evidenced by the Forces Determining Its Ordinances, 1935-1941" (Ph.D. dissertation, Indiana University, 1943), 197-98; and Wes Gehring, "The Patriotic Last Days of Carole Lombard," *Traces of Indiana and Midwestern History* 14 (spring 2002): 4-15.

10. James B. Lane, *"City of the Century": A History of Gary, Indiana* (Bloomington.: Indiana University Press, 1978), 212; Richard M. Ugland, "Viewpoints and Morale of Urban High School Students during World War II—Indianapolis as a Case Study," *Indiana Magazine of History* 78 (1981): 150-78; James H. Madison, *A Lynching in the Heartland: Race and Memory in America* (New York: Palgrave/St. Martins, 2001), 118; Marian K. Towne, *That All May Be One: Centennial History of Church Women United in Indianapolis, 1898-1998* (Indianapolis: Church Women United, 1998), 42-43; Thornbrough and Ruegamer, *Indiana Blacks in the Twentieth Century*, 99.

11. Gerald F. Linderman, *The World Within War: America's Combat Experience in World War II* (New York: The Free Press, 1997), 300-44; George H. Roeder Jr., *The Censored War: American Visual Experience During World War Two* (New Haven: Yale University Press, 1993), 2-5, 52; Paul Fussell, *Wartime: Understanding and Behavior in the Second World War* (New York: Oxford University Press, 1989); James Allison, "Mutiny at Freeman Field: The Life and the Art of James Gould Cozzens," *Black History News and Notes* 92 (May 2003): 4-7; Ray Boomhower, "'Nobody Wanted Us': Black Aviators at Freeman Field," *Traces of Indiana and Midwestern History* 5 (summer 1993): 38-45.

12. Fussell, *Wartime*, 145-46; Linderman, *The World Within War*, 302-4; Howard H. Peckham and Shirley A. Snyder, eds., *Letters from Fighting Hoosiers* (Bloomington: Indiana War History Commission, 1948), 183-84.

13. Ernie Pyle, *Brave Men* (New York: Henry Holt and Co., 1944), 106-107; James Tobin, *Ernie Pyle's War: America's Eyewitness to World War II* (New York: The Free Press, 1997), 109-13, 139-43, 243 (Miller quote); Linderman, *The World Within War*, 324-26, 325 (letter to Eisenhower).

14. Quoted in Tobin, *Ernie Pyle's War*, 4.

15. Frederick S. Voss, *Reporting the War: The Journalistic Coverage of World War II* (Washington, D.C.: National Portrait Gallery, Smithsonian Institution Press, 1994).

16. Clayton R. Koppes and Gregory D. Black, *Hollywood Goes to War: How Politics, Profits, and Propaganda Shaped World War II Movies* (Berkeley: University of California Press, 1987), 142-84; Thomas Doherty, *Projections of War: Hollywood, American Culture, and World War II* (New York: Columbia University Press, 1993); Lary May, *The Big Tomorrow: Hollywood and the Politics of the American Way* (Chicago: University of Chicago Press, 2000),139-74; Linderman, *World Within War*, 311-12; Peter Maslowski, *Armed with Cameras: The American Military Photographers of World War II* (New York: The Free Press, 1993), 67.

17. Roeder, *The Censored War*, 10-15, 56-58; Fussell, *Wartime*, 268-73; Maslowski, *Armed with Cameras*, 78-83. Ernie Pyle's references to race tended to be of the sort that didn't acknowledge segregation, as in his description of the cabin he shared with a fellow Hoosier on board a Navy carrier in the Pacific: "In our cabin we had metal closets and writing desks and a lavatory with hot and cold water We had a telephone and a colored boy to clean up the room." Ernie Pyle, *Last Chapter* (New York: Henry Holt and Co., 1945), 66.

18. Peckham and Snyder, *Letters from Fighting Hoosiers*, 244.

19. John W. Dower, *War Without Mercy: Race and Power in the Pacific War* (New York: Pantheon Books, 1986), 60-73; Peter Schrijvers, *The GI War Against Japan: American Soldiers in Asia and the Pacific During World War II* (New York: New York University Press, 2002), 165-83, 207-25; Lee Kennett, *G.I.: The American Soldier in World War II* (New York: Scribner, 1987), 162-68, 184-90; E. B. Sledge, *With the Old Breed at Peleliu and Okinawa* (Novato, Calif: Presidio Press, 1981), 120-21, 198-99.

20. Fussell, *Wartime*, ix, 142.

21. Bernard L. Rice, "Recollections of a World War II Combat Medic," *Indiana Magazine of History* 93 (December 1997): 344; James H. Madison, "World War II in Memory," *Indiana Magazine of History* 93 (December 1997): 309-11; Kurt Vonnegut Jr., *Slaughterhouse-five: Or, The Children's Crusade, a Duty-Dance with Death* (New York: Delacorte Press, 1969); Sledge, *With the Old Breed*. Vonnegut did share some of his story with his Indianapolis family in a powerful letter written May 29, 1945, and reprinted in *Traces of Indiana and Midwestern History* 3 (fall 1991): 43-45.

22. For an explicit black and white comparison of the two wars, see the back cover of the paperback version of Ernie Pyle, *Here Is Your War* (New York: Lancer Books, 1971): "The Old America—and the New. Then—A nation unified by a common morality and a common cause, fighting to salvage a world in flames and win the greatest war ever fought. Now—A nation seen by many as torn by moral and political dissent, seeking its salvation in riots, assassinations, new moralities, and drugs."

JOHN A. BUSHEMI: A BIOGRAPHY

1. Merle Miller, "Surprise Party at Eniwetok," *Yank*, March 3, 1944.

2. See James B. Lane, *"City of the Century": A History of Gary, Indiana* (Bloomington: Indiana University Press, 1978), 219; "'Johnny's' Buddy in Gary to Tell Story of Ace Photog's 'Last Fight,'" *Gary Post-Tribune*, April 7, 1944; and Art Weithas, *Close to Glory: The Untold Stories of WWII by the GIs Who Saw and Reported the War—YANK MAGAZINE Correspondents* (Austin: Eakin Press, 1991), xxv. The three other Yank staff members killed in the war were Basil D. Gallagher, who died in a plane crash in Brazil; Pete Paris, mortally wounded during the D-Day invasion; and Robert Krell, killed during an airborne operation on the Rhine River in Germany. See Weithas, *Close to Glory*, xxv.

3. See "John Bushemi," in Weithas, *Close to Glory*, 145.

4. "'One-Shot' Bushemi, Front Line Photog," *Gary Post-Tribune*, March 1, 1944.

5. See James B. Lane, "P-T Photog Became Top Gary War Hero," *Gary Post-Tribune*, August 3, 1975, and Lane, *"City of the Century*," 216, 218.

6. Also inducted with Bushemi into the Hall of Fame in 2001 were Frank Reynolds, ABC television newsman; Pat Siddons, retired publisher of the *Indiana Daily Student*; and Juliet Strauss, a noted columnist for the *Ladies' Home Journal* during the 1900s. See Indiana Journalism Hall of Fame website, http://www.newspaper.depauw.edu/halloffame/.

7. "'One-Shot' Johnny Bushemi Is Disappointed in Battle," *Gary Post-Tribune*, December 18, 1943. *Yank* correspondent Mack Morriss, who witnessed Roosevelt's visit to Guadalcanal with Bushemi, noted that during the First Lady's stop on the island "guys waved at a woman in a red cross uniform and ill [sic] bet no one in 100 knew it was mrs. Roosevelt, nor gave a damn so long as it was a woman. she was her usual smiling self, and very feminine in that she had that talk which ended in a laugh, in that her hose wrinkled and a bit of white slip showed on the left side." See Mack Morriss, New Georgia Diary, page 40. The diary belongs to Morriss's widow, Helen Morriss Wildasin of Elizabethton, Tennessee.

8. Marion Hargrove, "Last Assignment: Yank's Ace Photographer Johnny Bushemi Killed in Action," *US Camera*, May 1944, p. 55.

9. Kevin Cessna genealogy files.

10. Ibid.

11. Author interview with Mary Ellen and Kevin Cessna, March 27, 2002, Valparaiso, Indiana.

12. Ibid. See also *Times Capsule: The Times' History of the Calumet Region During the 20th Century* (Crown Point: Northwest Indiana Newspapers, 1999), 122.

13. See "Dedication" Program, Indiana News Photographers Association, April 19, 1958, French Lick, Indiana. Bushemi received a posthumous life membership from the INPA on April 19, 1958.

14. "'One-Shot' Bushemi, Front Line Photog," *Gary Post-Tribune*, March 1, 1944.

15. *Times Capsule*, 121.

16. Lisa Shidler, "The Legend of 'Johnny One Shot,'" *Gary Post-Tribune*, April 1, 2001.

17. "Burly Rail Cop Assaults Photog at Scene of Wreck," undated *Gary Post-Tribune* newspaper clipping, which is among the letters, photographs, and other material collected on Bushemi's life by his sister, Mary Ellen Cessna, Valparaiso, Indiana. Hereafter, this collection will be cited as Bushemi Papers.

18. Fort Benjamin Harrison served as the induction center for the Fifth Army Corps, which included the states of Indiana, Kentucky, Ohio, and West Virginia. The fort's reception center, which opened in time for the second group of draftees who arrived on January 14, 1941, included a classification section where inductees took intelligence and aptitude tests and were interviewed to ascertain their best fit in the army. After testing, draftees were sent to other bases in the country for basic training. See Max Parvin Cavnes, *The Hoosier Community at War* (Bloomington: Indiana University Press, 1961), 407, and Dorothy Riker, *The Hoosier Training Ground* (Bloomington: Indiana War History Commission, 1952), 169-70.

19. Hargrove, "Last Assignment," 11.

20. Ibid. See also author telephone interview with Hargrove, April 8, 2002.

21. Hargrove, "Last Assignment," 11-12. See also Marion Hargrove, *See Here, Private Hargrove* (New York: Henry Holt and Company, 1942), 132-34, and Hargrove interview.

22. Hargrove interview.

23. See Hargrove, *See Here, Private Hargrove*, 166-67, and Hargrove interview.

24. Ibid., 133-34. See also John Bushemi to Marion Hargrove, undated letter, Marion Hargrove Papers, Steele Memorial Library Branch, Wayne County Public Library, Mount Olive, North Carolina.

25. Maxwell Anderson, foreword, in *See Here, Private Hargrove*, ix-xi. See also Alfred S. Shivers, *Maxwell Anderson* (Twayne Publishers: Boston, 1976), 58, and Shivers, *The Life of Maxwell Anderson* (New York: Stein and Day, 1983), 193. Hargrove wrote Bushemi quoting Sloane as saying that the photographs Bushemi shot for the book were "perfectly marvelous. The guy is a real photographer. Heaven knows what he would do if he had a real subject to work with!" Marion Hargrove to John Bushemi, April 9, 1942, Bushemi Papers.

26. See Shivers, *Life of Maxwell Anderson*, 190, and Hargrove interview. Born in New York City, Shearer had been a reporter in Durham, North Carolina, before being drafted into the army. In addition to writing for *Yank* during the war, Shearer covered the Pacific theater for Armed Forces Radio. After the war he became a regular contributor to the *New York Times Magazine* and *Readers' Digest*. Shearer won enduring fame, however, for producing the "Personality Parade" column for *Parade* magazine under the pen name Walter Scott. He pro-duced the weekly column from 1958 until 1991, when Parkinson's disease forced him to stop. See Joyce Wadler, "Lloyd Shearer, Longtime Celebrity Columnist, Dies at 84," *New York Times*, May 27, 2001, and Elaine Woo, "Lloyd Shearer; Leader of the 'Personality Parade,'" *Los Angeles Times*, May 26, 2001.

27. Shivers, *Life of Maxwell Anderson*, 192. See also Hargrove interview, and Hargrove, "Last Assignment," 13. Period accounts of the incident, especially those written by Shearer, detailed a more violent awakening for Anderson, with some accounts having Bishop actually kick Anderson in the thigh. Even Hargove wrote that an embarrassed Bishop avoided the playwright for the rest of the day. See Shivers, *Life of Maxwell Anderson*, 193, and Hargrove, "Last Assignment," 13.

28. Lloyd Shearer, "Pertaining to Local Color," *New York Times*, October 4, 1942.

29. Maxwell Anderson to Edwin P. Parker Jr., March 11, 1942, in Laurence G. Avery, ed., *Dramatist in America: Letters of Maxwell Anderson, 1912-1958* (Chapel Hill: University of North Carolina Press, 1977), 120. See also Shivers, *Life of Maxwell Anderson*, 193, 332.

30. See Shivers, *Maxwell Anderson: An Annotated Bibliography of Primary and Secondary Works* (Metuchen, N.J.: The Scarecrow Press, 1985), 20. The play's title comes from a legend that states on the Eve of St. Mark a virgin can stand at a church door and view all those in a community who will die during the year. If by chance her lover is among those who are destined to die, he will look at her and perhaps even speak. In addition to the soldiers he met at Fort Bragg, Anderson based his work in part on the life of his nephew Chambers.

31. Shearer, "Pertaining to Local Color," *New York Times*. One Anderson biographer has noted that the character based on Hargrove (Francis Marion) proved to be so charming and humorous that he "threatens to steal audience interest away from the [play's] nominal hero, Quizz West." See Shivers, *Maxwell Anderson: An Annotated Bibliography*, 21.

32. Shearer, "Pertaining to Local Color," *New York Times*. See also Shivers, *Maxwell Anderson*, 59, and Anderson, *The Eve of St. Mark* (Chicago: Dramatic Publishing Company, 1942), 99. Hollywood also became attracted to Hargrove's view of army life. In 1944 Metro-Goldwyn-Mayer released *See Here, Private Hargrove*, a movie based on the soldier's book and starring Robert Walker as the title character and Keenan Wynn as Private Mulvehill. Although a character based on Bushemi had been planned to be included in the movie, the necessary release papers failed to reach the photographer in time for filming. See Cessna interview and *See Here, Private Hargrove* entry, Internet Movie Database, http://us.imdb.com/Title ?0037256.

33. Hargrove interview. The son of a Methodist minister and author of the popular book *One Foot in Heaven*, Spence was one of the four people who helped design a dummy edition of *Yank* for presentation to Secretary of War Henry L. Stimson. The others involved in designing the issue were Weithas, an advertising art director; Newt Oliphant, a songwriter; Ralph

Stein, a cartoonist; Guy Tuamburo, a type designer; Egbert White, an advertising executive; and Franklin S. Forsberg, an executive with Street and Smith publications. As *Yank*'s executive editor, Spence is often credited with coining the term "pinup" for the photographs of scantily clad film stars he used in the magazine. He also discovered George Baker, who produced the popular "Sad Sack" cartoon for the magazine. See Weithas, *Close to Glory*, 3, and Jon Thurber, "Hartzell Spence—Pioneer of Pinups," *San Francisco Chronicle*, May 29, 2001.

34. Joe McCarthy, "The Difference Between Stars and Stripes and Yank," *Saturday Review*, July 7, 1945. See also Annie Davis Weeks, Introduction, *Yank, The Army Weekly* (New York: New York Public Library, 1950), 5. The casual atmosphere at *Yank* in its early days horrified army officials. After receiving complaints from the War Department about the magazine's "unmilitary attitude," a more regular army routine was established for the magazine's staff. A regular drill routine was instituted and those who arrived late had to wash the office walls.

35. Alfred E. Cornebise, *Ranks and Columns: Armed Forces Newspapers in American Wars* (Westport, Conn.: Greenwood Press, 1993), 138-39, and Editorial, *Yank*, June 17, 1942, p. 15. See also Dave Richardson, "YANK Magazine GI Photographers Cover Every Front World War II," *Captions: International Combat Camera Association, Inc.* (fall 2000): 4.

36. Hargrove, "Last Assignment," 51, and Hargrove interview.

37. Undated article by Vicktor Keppler, "The Yank Is Coming," Bushemi Papers.

38. Weithas, *Close to Glory*, 4-5.

39. John Bushemi letter to Mary Ellen Bushemi, October 10, 1942, Bushemi Papers. British actress Madeleine Carroll appeared in such films as Alfred Hitchcock's *The 39 Steps* (1935), *Secret Agent* (1936), and *The Prisoner of Zenda* (1937). See also "Gals Behind the Guns," *Yank*, September 16, 1942; Bill Davidson, "Desert Warfare: America Trains a New Kind of Army," *Yank*, September 23, 1942; and Walter Bernstein, "Benning School for Boys," *Yank*, October 21, 1942.

40. Memo to Franklin Forsberg from Hartzell Spence, September 5, 1942, Joe McCarthy Papers in George Burns Collection, U.S. Military History Institute, Carlisle Barracks, Carlisle, Pennsylvania (hereafter cited as McCarthy Papers).

41. "Johnny Gets Poetic (Almost) in Describing Trip to Hawaii," *Gary Post-Tribune*, December 30, 1942.

42. Ibid.

43. Merle Miller to Hartzell Spence, November 18, 1942, McCarthy Papers, U.S. Military History Institute.

44. See Miller, "Hawaii's Hillbillies," *Yank*, December 30, 1942; Miller, "Hooper's Troopers," *Yank*, January 13, 1943; "Pigeoneers," cover photograph, *Yank*, March 5, 1943; and Miller, "How to Live on a Desert Island," *Yank*, May 21, 1943.

45. Bushemi to Hargrove, December 12, 1942, Hargrove Papers, Steele Memorial Library.

46. See Hargrove, "Last Assignment," 51, and Spence to Miller, February 19, 1943, McCarthy Papers, U.S. Military History Institute. See also "Gary's Johnny One Shot Promoted

on Yank Staff," *Gary Post-Tribune*, June 23, 1943. Miller later covered the European theater for *Yank*, earning a Bronze Star for his efforts. After the war he worked for *Time* and *Harper's* before embarking on a freelance career as a writer of fiction and nonfiction. Miller, who confessed his homosexuality in a groundbreaking 1971 article for the *New York Times Magazine*, achieved his greatest success through his work as a researcher and writer for a planned television series on President Harry Truman. Although the project failed, Miller used his experience with Truman to produce the best-selling *Plain Speaking: An Oral Biography of Harry S. Truman* (1974). Miller died on June 10, 1986. See W. Farrell O'Gorman, "Merle Miller," in John A. Garraty and Mark C. Carnes, *American National Biography* (New York: Oxford University Press, 1999), 507-8.

47. "'Johnny' Buddy in Gary to Tell Story of Ace Photog's 'Last Fight,'" *Gary Post-Tribune*, April 7, 1944.

48. See Miller, "John Bushemi, KIA," in Weithas, *Close to Glory*, 150.

49. John A. Bushemi to Frank Bushemi, February 27, 1943, Bushemi Papers.

50. Miller to Spence, February 11, 1943, McCarthy Papers, U.S. Military History Institute.

51. Captain Reginald Jackson, "Yanks I Have Known," McCarthy Papers, U.S. Military History Institute.

52. Miller to Spence, May 9, 1943, McCarthy Papers, U.S. Military History Institute.

53. Ronnie Day, ed., *Mack Morriss, South Pacific Diary, 1942-1943* (Lexington: The University Press of Kentucky, 1996), 194.

54. Miller to Spence, June 16, 1943, McCarthy Papers, U.S. Military History Institute.

55. Ibid.

56. Morriss, *South Pacific Diary*, 243, note 6. See also Morriss to Spence, August 19, 1943, McCarthy Papers, U.S. Military History Institute. In his letter to Spence from Munda, New Georgia, Morriss wrote that he and Bushemi planned on "doing as much as possible here within a short length of time and then moving on." He noted that the territory around Munda Airfield was the worst he had ever seen in the Pacific, "bombed and shelled to a shambles." American forces were fighting through country that easily compared "with the worst on Guadalcanal," Morriss wrote.

57. Hargrove, "Last Assignment," 51. See also Susan D. Moeller, *Shooting War: Photography and the American Experience of Combat* (New York: Basic Books, 1989), 194.

58. See William Manchester, *American Caesar: Douglas McCarthur, 1880-1964* (Boston: Little, Brown and Co., 1978), 278; Manchester, *Goodbye Darkness: A Memoir of the Pacific War* (Boston: Little, Brown and Co., 1979), 252-53; and Ronald H. Spector, *Eagle Against the Sun: The American War with Japan* (New York: The Free Press, 1985), 247.

59. Morriss, New Georgia Diary, 24-25.

60. Keith Crown, "Johnny Bushemi," McCarthy Papers, U.S. Military History Institute. Crown learned of Bushemi's death

after reading "one of those three-sheet mimeographed newspapers that are characteristic of the U.S. Army."

61. In 1970 Keith Crown Sr. was inducted into the Indiana Basketball Hall of Fame. Crown coached basketball at Horace Mann for forty years, served as an early president of the Indiana High School Coaches Association, and refereed more than one thousand high school basketball games. See Indiana Basketball Hall of Fame website, http://www.hoopshall.com/inductees/1970/crown.html.

62. Crown, "Johnny Bushemi," McCarthy Papers, U.S. Military History Institute.

63. Morriss, New Georgia Diary, 46–47.

64. "'One-Shot' Johnny Bushemi Is Disappointed in Battle," *Gary Post-Tribune*, December 18, 1943.

65. Morriss, New Georgia Diary, 48. *Yank* staff were quite used to being accused by those involved in the fighting as having it easy. Bill McGurn, a reporter for the *New York Herald Tribune* prior to joining *Yank*, was covering the action on Bougainville for the magazine when he was wounded by Japanese mortar fire. After his initial treatment by medics, McGurn, still queasy from his ordeal, sat next to a marine who turned to him and asked: "Is it true? Are you with *Yank*? What a racket!" See Weithas, *Close to Glory*, 131–34.

66. Joe McCarthy to Charles Balthrope, September 29, 1943, McCarthy Papers, U.S. Military History Institute.

67. Morriss, *South Pacific Diary*, 243, note 6. Looking back on the three and a half years he spent working for *Yank*, Morriss observed: "The experience—whether it was living it up in Paris or London or New York or Honolulu or Auckland, New Zealand, or sweating it out in a foxhole in the Solomons or Germany or on some rock of an island with one tree 7,000 miles from home, or up 20,000 feet in a B-17, or on an LST headed for a new beach, or in a hospital with a guy shivering with malaria and a backful of grenade fragments, or in a wrecked schoolhouse with a dead GI in the doorway, or looking at a guy standing in the door of a battalion aid station with an arm blown off, or looking at a man in the floor crying, or simply pulling guard on the motor pool with frost glistening in the moonlight—the experience had a lasting effect on me: It made me believe in this country and in us Americans." Ibid., 4.

68. Bushemi to McCarthy, October 9, 1943, McCarthy Papers, U.S. Military History Institute.

69. See Holland M. Smith, *Coral and Brass* (New York: Charles Scribner's Sons, 1949), 125; *The Capture of Makin, 20-24 November 1943* (1946; reprint, Washington, D.C.: Center of Military History, United States Army, 1990), 93–94; and Samuel Eliot Morison, *History of United States Naval Operations in World War II, Vol. 7: Aleutians, Gilberts and Marshalls, June 1942-April 1944* (Boston: Little, Brown and Co., 1961), 122. The American forces were even "trigger happy" during daylight hours. On one occasion, a soldier from the 152nd Engineers ran along Makin's lagoon shore shouting: "There's a hundred and fifty Japs in the trees." The false statement resulted in a wave of shooting that could only be stopped after direct commands to individual soldiers. *The Capture of Makin*, 95.

70. Bushemi to Morriss, January 2, 1944, McCarthy Papers, U.S. Military History Institute.

71. See "Funeral Service for 'Johnny' Friday," *Gary Post-Tribune*, March 2, 1944; *The Capture of Makin*, 118–20; and Morison, *History of United States Naval Operations in World War II, Vol. 7: Aleutians, Gilberts and Marshalls*, 134.

72. Robert Sherrod, *Tarawa: The Story of a Battle* (1944; reprint, Fredericksburg, Texas: Admiral Nimitz Foundation, 1973), 149.

73. "'Johnny's' Buddy in Gary to Tell Story of Ace Photog's 'Last Fight,'" *Gary Post-Tribune*.

74. "Funeral Service for 'Johnny' Friday," *Gary Post-Tribune*, March 2, 1944.

75. Bushemi to Morriss, January 2, 1944, McCarthy Papers, U.S. Military History Institute.

76. John Bushemi, "Death Battle at Tarawa," *Yank*, December 24, 1943.

77. McCarthy to Bushemi, undated, McCarthy Papers, U.S. Military History Institute.

78. Bushemi to Morriss, January 2, 1944, McCarthy Papers, U.S. Military History Institute.

79. Hargrove, "Last Assignment," 51.

80. Forsberg to Bushemi, January 11, 1943, Bushemi Papers, and McCarthy to Bushemi, January 15, 1944, McCarthy Papers, U.S. Military History Institute.

81. Peter Maslowski, *Armed with Cameras: The American Military Photographers of World War II* (New York: The Free Press, 1993), 47–48.

82. Morriss, *New Georgia Diary*, 10.

83. Bushemi to McCarthy, January 9, 1944, McCarthy Papers, U.S. Military History Institute.

84. See Spector, *Eagle Against the Sun*, 268–71; Morison, *History of United States Naval Operations in World War II, Vol. 7: Aleutians, Gilberts and Marshalls*, 230–81; and Philip A. Crowl and Edmund G. Love, *United States Army in World War II: The War in the Pacific: Seizure of the Gilberts and Marshalls* (Washington, D.C.: Office of the Chief of Military History, Department of the Army, 1955), 175–82.

85. Bushemi, "Kwajalein Report and Pacific Strategy," in Weithas, *Close to Glory*, 146–48.

86. Charles R. Vandergrift to Balthrope, March 1, 1944, Bushemi Papers. See also Morison, *History of United States Naval Operations in World War II, Vol. 7: Aleutians, Gilberts and Marshalls*, 236–40.

87. Bushemi, "Kwajalein Report and Pacific Strategy," *Close to Glory*, 148. In his report to McCarthy Bushemi also sent his regards to the rest of the *Yank* staff and asked about a secretary at the office. "I would like her if she's built like you say she is," he told McCarthy. "What the hell does she look like? I understand she moves around and her blood circulates."

88. "'Johnny's' Buddy in Gary to Tell Story of Ace Photog's 'Last Fight,'" *Gary Post-Tribune*, April 7, 1944. Miller's article on the reconnaissance troops, along with Bushemi's photographs, appeared in *Yank*'s March 17, 1944, issue as "First Yanks on Jap Soil."

89. See James H. McConnell to Bushemi family, August 4, 1944, Bushemi Papers, and "Johnny's Buddy in Gary to Tell Story of Ace Photog's 'Last Fight,'" *Gary Post-Tribune*, April 7, 1944.

90. Miller, "Surprise Party on Eniwetok," *Yank*.

91. Ibid., and "Jap Shell Ends Life of Gary Photo 'Ace,'" *Gary Post-Tribune*, March 1, 1944.

92. Gus Mitchell article on Bushemi's death dated April 8, 1997, in Bushemi Papers. Seriously wounded during the invasion of Saipan, Mitchell was evacuated to a hospital in Hawaii. While recuperating in the hospital he picked up an issue of *Yank* and learned of Bushemi's death. "Not enough can be said about these brave Reporters and Photographers that scarify [*sic*] their lives just to get a picture and a story to let everyone know how the war is being fought and the men that fight them," wrote Mitchell. "I think that they are all hero's, armed with only a Camera, a pencil and a piece of paper to write a story about a war. My hat is off to them."

93. "Johnny's Buddy in Gary to Tell Story of Ace Photog's 'Last Fight,'" *Gary Post-Tribune*, April 7, 1944.

94. See Miller, "Surprise Party at Eniwetok," and "'Johnny's' Buddy in Gary to Tell Story of Ace Photog's 'Last Fight,'" *Gary Post-Tribune*, April 7, 1944.

95. See Miller, "Burial at Sea," in Weithas, *Close to Glory*, 150, and "'Johnny's' Buddy in Gary to Tell Story of Ace Photog's 'Last Fight,'" *Gary Post-Tribune*.

96. Major General J. A. Ulio telegram to Peter Bushemi, February 29, 1944, Bushemi Papers.

97. McCarthy to Yank Correspondents Overseas, Letter No. 48, March 2, 1944, Hargrove Papers, Steele Memorial Library.

98. Miller to Robert Greenhalgh, March 1, 1944, McCarthy Papers, U.S. Military History Institute.

99. Miller to Morriss, March 7, 1944, McCarthy Papers, U.S. Military History Institute.

100. Hargrove to Mary Ellen Bushemi, March 1, 1944, Bushemi Papers.

101. Lloyd Shearer to Bushemi family, March 1, 1944, Bushemi Papers.

102. Morriss to Bushemi family, March 2, 1944, Bushemi Papers.

103. Mary Ellen Bushemi to Hargrove, March 10, 1944, Hargrove Papers, Steele Memorial Library.

104. Erwin Crewe Rosenau "Gary Mourns at Memorial for 'Johnny,'" *Gary Post-Tribune*, March 3, 1944.

105. See "Bushemi's Photographs! 200 of Ace Cameraman's Pictures Go on Display Sunday in Gary Library," *Gary Post-Tribune*, April 29, 1944; "New Award to Bushemi for Heroism," *Gary Post-Tribune*, June 14, 1944; and Bronze Star award, Bushemi Papers.

106. See "Bodies Arrive," *Gary Post-Tribune*, October 10, 1947; "Bushemi Post to Honor Hero at Last Rites," *Gary Post-Tribune*, November 1, 1947; and "Friends Pay Final Honor to Bushemi," *Gary Post-Tribune*, November 5, 1947.

107. See Cessna interview and Shidler, "The Legend of 'Johnny One Shot,'" *Gary Post-Tribune*, April 1, 2001.

SELECT BIBLIOGRAPHY

BOOKS

Avery, Laurence G., ed. *Dramatist in America: Letters of Maxwell Anderson, 1912-1958*. Chapel Hill: University of North Carolina Press, 1977.

The Best from YANK The Army Weekly. Cleveland: The World Publishing Company, 1945.

The Capture of Makin, 20-24 November 1943. 1946. Reprint, Washington, D.C.: Center of Military History, U.S. Army, 1990.

Cavnes, Max Parvin. *The Hoosier Community at War*. Bloomington: Indiana University Press, 1961.

Cornebise, Alfred E. *Ranks and Columns: Armed Forces Newspapers in American Wars*. Westport, Conn.: Greenwood Press, 1993.

Crowl, Philip A. and Edmund G. Love. *United States Army in World War II: The War in the Pacific: The Seizure of the Gilberts and Marshalls*. Washington, D.C.: Office of the Chief of Military History, Department of the Army, 1955.

Day, Ronnie, ed. *South Pacific Diary, 1942-1943*. Lexington: The University Press of Kentucky, 1996.

Dornbusch, C.E. *Yank, the Army Weekly: A Check List*. New York: New York Public Library, 1950.

Hargrove, Marion. *See Here, Private Hargrove*. New York: Henry Holt and Company, 1942.

Kluger, Steve. *Yank: The Army Weekly: World War II from the Guys Who Brought You Victory*. New York: St. Martin's Press, 1990.

Lane, James B. *"City of the Century": A History of Gary, Indiana*. Bloomington: Indiana University Press, 1978.

Manchester, William. *Goodbye Darkness: A Memoir of the Pacific War*. Boston: Little, Brown and Company, 1979.

_____. *American Caesar: Douglas McCarthur, 1880-1964*. Boston: Little, Brown and Company, 1978.

Maslowski, Peter. *Armed with Cameras: The American Military Photographers of World War II*. New York: The Free Press, 1993.

Moeller, Susan D. *Shooting War: Photography and the American Experience of Combat*. New York: Basic Books, 1989.

Morison, Samuel Eliot. *History of United States Naval Operations in World War II, Vol. 7: Aleutians, Gilberts and Marshalls, June 1942-April 1944*. Boston: Little, Brown and Company, 1961.

Moyes, Norman B. *Battle Eye: A History of American Combat Photography*. New York: MetroBooks, 1996.

O'Gorman, W. Farrell "Merle Miller," in John A. Garraty and Mark C. Carnes, *American National Biography* (New York: Oxford University Press, 1999).

Riker, Dorothy. *The Hoosier Training Ground*. Bloomington: Indiana War History Commission, 1952.

Sherrod, Robert. *Tarawa: The Story of a Battle*. 1944. Reprint, Fredericksburg, Texas: Admiral Nimitz Foundation, 1973.

Shivers, Alfred S. *Maxwell Anderson*. Boston: Twayne Publishers, 1976.

_____. *Maxwell Anderson: An Annotated Bibliography of Primary and Secondary Works*. Metuchen, N.J.: The Scarecrow Press, 1985.

_____. *The Life of Maxwell Anderson*. New York: Stein and Day, 1983.

Smith, Holland M. and Percy Finch. *Coral and Brass*. New York: Charles Scribner's Sons, 1949.

Spector, Ronald H. *Eagle Against the Sun: The American War with Japan*. New York: The Free Press, 1985.

Times Capsule: The Times' History of the Calumet Region during the 20th Century. Crown Point: Northwest Indiana Newspapers, 1999.

Weithas, Art. *Close to Glory: The Untold Stories of WWII by the GIs Who Saw and Reported the War—YANK Magazine Correspondents.* Austin: Eakin Press, 1991.

PERIODICALS, MANUSCRIPTS, AND INTERVIEWS

Bushemi, John. "Death Battle at Tarawa," *Yank*, December 24, 1943.

Cessna, Mary Ellen and Kevin Cessna. Interview with Ray E. Boomhower, March 27, 2002, Valparaiso, Indiana.

Hargrove, Marion. Papers. Steele Memorial Library Branch, Wayne County Public Library, Mount Olive, North Carolina.

_____. Telephone interview with Ray E. Boomhower, April 8, 2002.

_____. "Last Assignment: Yank's Ace Photographer Johnny Bushemi Killed in Action." *US Camera*, May 1944.

McCarthy, Joe. Papers. George Burns Collection, U.S. Military History Institute, Carlisle Barracks, Carlisle, Pennsylvania.

_____. "The Difference Between *Stars and Stripes* and *Yank.*" *Saturday Review*, July 7, 1945.

Miller, Merle. "Surprise Party at Eniwetok," *Yank*, March 3, 1944.

Morriss, Mack. New Georgia Diary. The diary belongs to Morriss's widow, Helen Morriss Wildasin, Elizabethton, Tennessee.

Richardson, Dave. "YANK Magazine GI Photographers Cover Every Front World War II," *Captions: International Combat Camera Association, Inc.* (fall 2000).

Shearer, Lloyd. "Pertaining to Local Color," *New York Times*, October 4, 1942.

Shidler, Lisa. "The Legend of 'Johnny One Shot,'" *Gary Post-Tribune*, April 1, 2001.

(ABOVE) **GI LOCKER AT THE FIELD ARTILLERY REPLACEMENT CENTER, FORT BRAGG, NORTH CAROLINA.**

MARY ELLEN CESSNA

(RIGHT) **BUSHEMI'S PHOTOGRAPH OF ROBERT CRYE OF RICHMOND, DUBBED "AMERICAN SOLDIER," APPEARED ON THE COVER OF THE JANUARY 1942 ISSUE OF THE *FIELD ARTILLERY JOURNAL*.**

MARY ELLEN CESSNA

(ABOVE) **CONSTRUCTION CREWS FORD A FLOODED
ROAD AT FORT BRAGG.**

MARY ELLEN CESSNA

(RIGHT) **RAY ADAMS (LEFT) AND IRVING SHEER PLANT KISSES
ON DINAH SHORE AFTER A PERFORMANCE AT FORT BRAGG.**

MARY ELLEN CESSNA

**TWO PHOTOGRAPHS OF HOLLYWOOD STAR MICKEY ROONEY
DURING A VISIT TO FORT BRAGG.**
MARY ELLEN CESSNA

(LEFT) **VERONICA LAKE IN A PUBLICITY SHOT FOR *YANK*.**

MARY ELLEN CESSNA

(ABOVE) **ACTRESS DIXIE DUNBAR.**

MARY ELLEN CESSNA

**TWO MEMBERS OF THE MUSICAL COMEDY "JUNIOR MISS" POSE WITH A 240MM HOWITZER
AFTER ENTERTAINING THE TROOPS AT THE FIELD ARTILLERY REPLACEMENT CENTER.**

MARY ELLEN CESSNA

**MRS. MARY FULTZ FIRES A .50 CALIBRE MACHINE GUN AT THE ABERDEEN PROVING
GROUNDS IN MARYLAND. THE PHOTOGRAPH APPEARED ON
THE COVER OF *YANK*'S SEPTEMBER 16, 1942, ISSUE.**

MARY ELLEN CESSNA

A SOLDIER SHAVES, GIS LEAP FROM A HALFTRACK, AND TANKS RUMBLE INTO ACTION IN CALIFORNIA'S MOJAVE DESERT IN A SERIES OF PHOTOGRAPHS BUSHEMI TOOK TO ILLUSTRATE BILL DAVIDSON'S ARTICLE "DESERT WARFARE: AMERICA TRAINS A NEW KIND OF ARMY," WHICH APPEARED IN *YANK*'S SEPTEMBER 23, 1942, ISSUE.

MARY ELLEN CESSNA

CORPORAL FRANCIS MITCHELL OF OMAHA, NEBRASKA, IS FIRED ON WHILE CROSSING A RAVINE AND ATTACKS A DUMMY WITH HIS BAYONET AS PART OF HIS TRAINING AT THE OFFICER CANDIDATE SCHOOL AT FORT BENNING, GEORGIA. BUSHEMI'S PHOTOGRAPHS ILLUSTRATED WALTER BERNSTEIN'S ARTICLE "BENNING SCHOOL FOR BOYS," WHICH APPEARED IN *YANK*'S OCTOBER 21, 1942, ISSUE. MITCHELL RECEIVED HIS COMMISSION AS A SECOND LIEUTENANT.

MARY ELLEN CESSNA

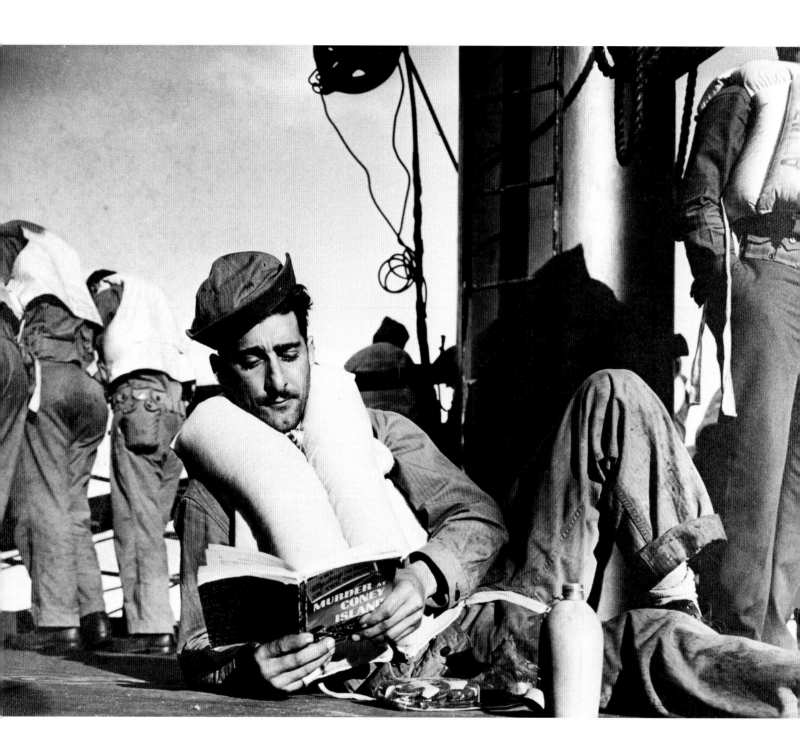

PRIVATE ALCIDEAS CHACON OF THE U.S. ARMY IS A MAN WHO CAN MAKE THE MOST OF ANY SITUATION—EVEN ABOARD A SHIP EN ROUTE TO A PACIFIC BASE. CHACON IS READING JAMES O'HANLON'S 1939 MYSTERY *MURDER AT CONEY ISLAND*.

MARY ELLEN CESSNA

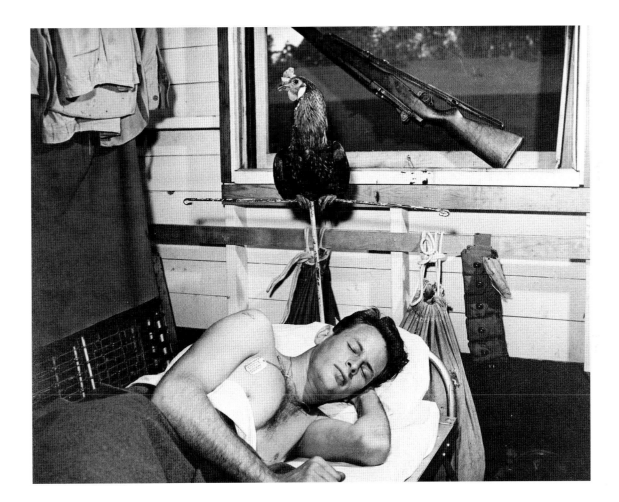

**RUMBOOGIE, THE ROOSTER MASCOT OF CORPORAL WILLIAM GEIGER OF NEW ORLEANS, WAKES
HIS MASTER IN HAWAII. BUSHEMI'S PHOTOGRAPH APPEARED ON THE COVER OF** *YANK'S*
FEBRUARY 14, 1943, BRITISH EDITION.

MARY ELLEN CESSNA

THREE MEMBERS OF COLONEL CHAUNCEY M. HOOPER'S ALL-BLACK COMBAT UNIT, "HOOPER'S
TROOPERS," SPLASH IN THE SURF IN HAWAII. BUSHEMI'S PHOTOGRAPHS APPEARED WITH
MERLE MILLER'S ARTICLE IN *YANK*'S JANUARY 13, 1943, ISSUE. THE PHOTOGRAPHER IDENTIFIED
THE SOLDIERS AS (LEFT TO RIGHT) CORPORAL PITTS, PRIVATE HENDRIX,
AND PRIVATE FIRST CLASS ROBINSON.

MARY ELLEN CESSNA

PRIVATE FIRST CLASS HARRY BOURASSA OF PERRY, FLORIDA, WAS ONE OF THE MULE SKINNERS IN THE ARMY'S HAWAIIAN PACK TRAIN PROFILED BY MILLER AND BUSHEMI IN *YANK'S* **DECEMBER 30, 1942, ISSUE. THE PHOTO OF BOURASSA APPEARED ON THE MAGAZINE'S COVER.**

MARY ELLEN CESSNA

(LEFT) **WAR DOG SIR ASSISTS TWO PIGEONEERS, PRIVATE FIRST CLASS CLAUDE SOWDEN** (LEFT)
AND SERGEANT ROWLAND FRENDO, IN TRAINING PIGEONS FOR ARMY WORK IN HAWAII.
SIR CARRIED THE BIRDS TO A MOUNTAIN POST WHERE THEY WERE RELEASED FOR THE FLIGHT
HOME. THE HAWAII PIGEON SECTION WAS PART OF THE SIGNAL CORPS. THE PIGEONS TRAINED
IN HAWAII WERE READY FOR ACTION AFTER TWO MONTHS OF TRAINING. THEY WERE USED TO
SEND DISTRESS MESSAGES, INCLUDING BEING RELEASED FROM BOMBERS. BUSHEMI'S
PHOTOGRAPH APPEARED ON THE COVER OF *YANK*'S **MARCH 5, 1943, ISSUE.**
MARY ELLEN CESSNA

(ABOVE) **A WOULD-BE MEMBER OF A MOUNTAIN RESCUE TEAM CLIMBS DOWN A MOUNTAIN IN**
HAWAII. DURING THE GROUP'S TWENTY-SIX-WEEK TRAINING PERIOD, ONE HALF OF THE
TRAINEES FAILED TO MAKE THE GRADE.
MARY ELLEN CESSNA

(LEFT) **STAFF SERGEANT CHARLES GARDOCKI KNOWS HOW TO GET THE MOST OUT OF A COCONUT TREE FOR CLOTHES, FOOD, AND SHELTER. BUSHEMI'S PHOTOGRAPH OF GARDOCKI APPEARED ON THE COVER OF** YANK'S **MAY 21, 1943, ISSUE WITH THE CAPTION "PIN-UP FOR WAAC'S."**

MARY ELLEN CESSNA

(ABOVE) **BUSHEMI'S PHOTOGRAPHS OF A GI ASSISTING AN ISLANDER IN THE FINE ART OF BUGLING AND A WOMAN NAMED MARGARET DOING LAUNDRY FOR AMERICAN SOLDIERS APPEARED IN A PHOTO SPREAD IN** YANK'S **DECEMBER 17, 1943, ISSUE UNDER THE TITLE "VISIT TO FIJI." THE BUGLER SHOT APPEARED ON THE MAGAZINE'S COVER.**

MARY ELLEN CESSNA

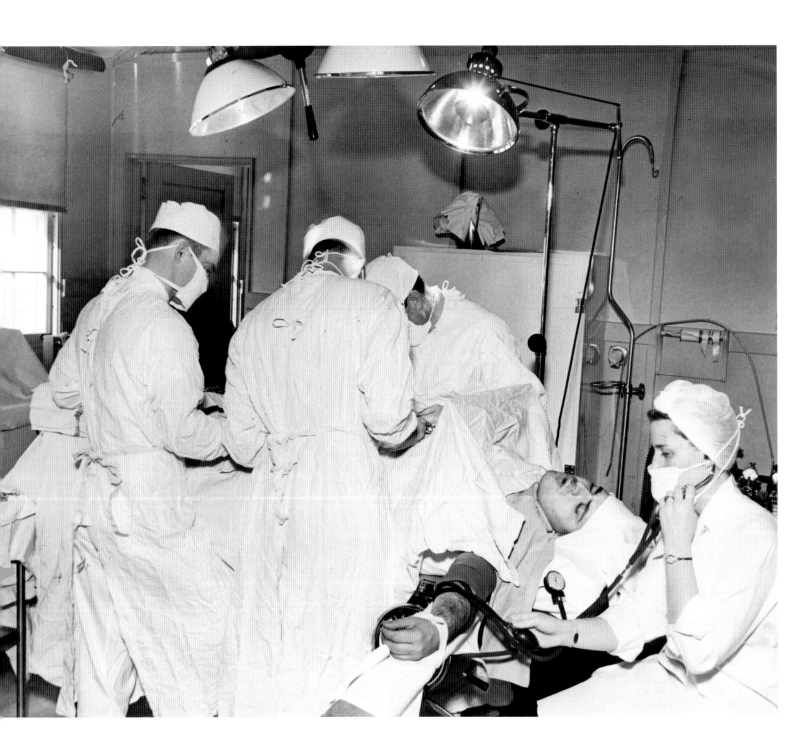

A SOLDIER UNDERGOES AN OPERATION AT AN UNIDENTIFIED ARMY BASE.
MARY ELLEN CESSNA

G. O. BACKBURN OF CHICAGO, ILLINOIS, SERVED AS A GUN CAPTAIN ON A LANDING SHIP, TANK (LST) SOMEWHERE OFF NEW GEORGIA. A NUMBER OF *YANK* STAFF MEMBERS MISTOOK BACKBURN FOR CHARACTER ACTOR ALAN HALE.

MARY ELLEN CESSNA

SERGEANT ARCHIE MCLEAN OF RHODES, MICHIGAN, LOOKS LIKE A MAN WHO HAS BEEN TO
THE WARS. AND HE HAS. ALREADY A VETERAN OF THE FIGHTING ON GUADALCANAL,
HE FOUGHT THE JAPANESE AGAIN ON NEW GEORGIA. IN THE BATTLE NEAR MUNDA,
MCLEAN'S SQUAD OF RIFLEMEN HAD THE JOB OF PROTECTING MACHINE GUN CREWS

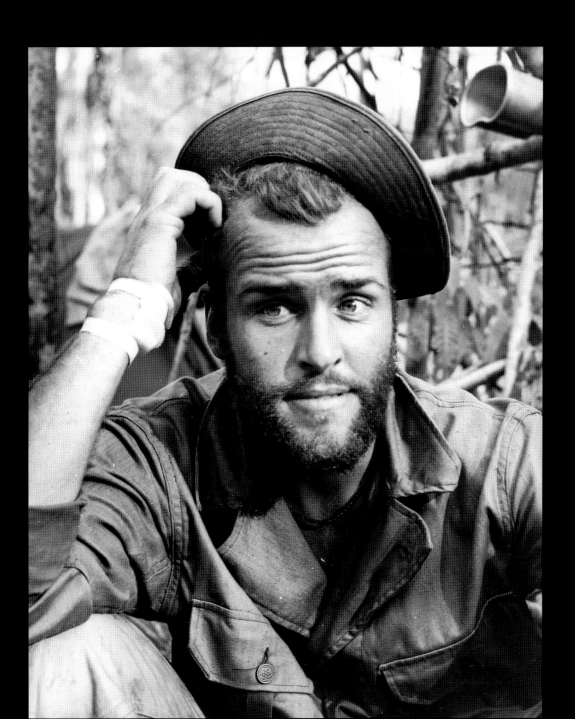

CAPTAIN DONALD DOWNEN OF PULLMAN, WASHINGTON, COMMANDING OFFICER OF
COMPANY A, WITH DUAL-PURPOSE ANTI-AIRCRAFT GUN CAPTURED BY HIS OUTFIT. THE GUNS
WERE FIRST MISTAKEN FOR FIELD PIECES SINCE ONLY MUZZLES AND UPRIGHT ELEVATION SHAFTS
WERE VISIBLE UNDER CAMOUFLAGE, AND THE AMERICANS THOUGHT THE SHAFTS WERE WHEELS.

PRIVATE FIRST CLASS WILEY HOWINGTON OF ASHEVILLE, NORTH CAROLINA, CLEANS THE M1 HE
USED IN WIPING OUT A JAPANESE ANTI-AIRCRAFT GUN CREW IN A DUGOUT AT MUNDA.

**SERGEANT ELMER McGLYNN OF SEATTLE, WASHINGTON, HELPED CUT DOWN SIX ENEMY
SOLDIERS WITH A BAR [BROWNING AUTOMATIC RIFLE] WHEN THEY TRIED TO WIPE OUT
A MACHINE GUN COVERING HIS PLATOON'S ADVANCE.**

LIEUTENANT COLONEL JOE KATSARSKY, COMMANDER OF THE INFANTRY BATTALION THAT DROVE A WEDGE THROUGH ENEMY POSITIONS TO THE SEA IN THE BATTLE FOR MUNDA AIRFIELD. HE'S FROM BATTLE CREEK, MICHIGAN.

PRIVATE FIRST CLASS HERBERT HATHCOAT WORKED IN A COAL MINE AT HANCEVILLE, ALABAMA. AT MUNDA HE ESCAPED A JAPANESE GRENADE THAT WOUNDED TWO OF HIS BUDDIES. HE LATER CAME CLOSE TO BEING RIPPED APART BY MACHINE-GUN FIRE.

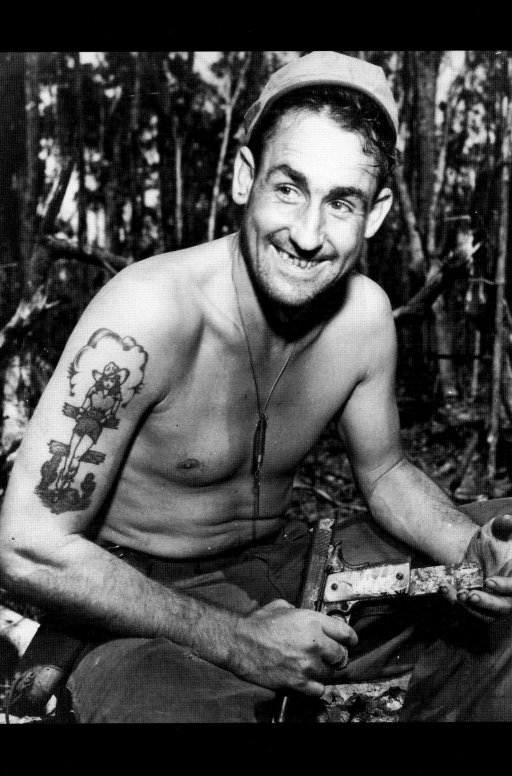

STAFF SERGEANT LEROY NORTON, THE EX-LUMBERJACK FROM BEND, OREGON, WHO WIPED OUT THREE JAPANESE IN A MACHINE-GUN EMPLACEMENT.

**STAFF SERGEANT CLARENCE TERRY, PLATOON LEADER FROM ARCO, IDAHO,
CLEANS HIS NAILS WITH A TRENCH KNIFE AFTER THE BATTLE AT HASTINGS RIDGE.**

TERRY DISPLAYS THE HELMET OF ERVIN BONOW AFTER A JAPANESE GRENADE HIT IT.
BONOW WAS LYING IN A HOLE, THE HELMET BETWEEN HIS LEGS, WHEN THE GRENADE LANDED.
HIS CALF MUSCLES WERE ALMOST COMPLETELY TORN AWAY.

STANDING KNEE DEEP IN SALTWATER UNDER THE BRANCHES OF A MANGO TREE, A WEAPONS COMPANY COMMANDER SPOTS BURSTS OF MORTAR FIRE.

**TWO GUNNERS GET THEIR LIGHT MACHINE GUN INTO PLACE BEHIND A FALLEN TREE AND WAIT
TO OPEN UP AT THE FIRST SIGN OF JAPANESE IN FRONT OF THEM.**

LIBRARY OF CONGRESS

**SOME WOUNDED ARE EVACUATED. SERGEANT D. S. JACKSON (LEFT) KILLED FIVE OF THE ENEMY
BEFORE HE WAS HIT. SERGEANT E. B. LOVETT'S HELMET WAS CREASED BY A BULLET.**

LIBRARY OF CONGRESS, LC-USZ62-19831

**CORPORAL LEWIS NIOVICH (LEFT) OF SEANOR, PENNSYLVANIA, AND STAFF SERGEANT
ANTHONY CAVALLERO OF WOODBRIDGE, NEW JERSEY, LIE BEHIND A LOG WITH AN
UNIDENTIFIED FELLOW SOLDIER AWAITING DEVELOPMENTS.**

LIBRARY OF CONGRESS, LC-USZ62-19828

**MEN WHO CALL THEMSELVES "SEAGOING ENGINEERS" PILOT SMALL FLAT-BOTTOMED BOATS
THROUGH THE ISLAND CHANNELS CARRYING MEN AND SUPPLIES.**

GIS WADE ACROSS THE ARUNDEL RIVER IN NEW GEORGIA.
LIBRARY OF CONGRESS, LC-USZ62-8713

A LIGHT MACHINE GUNNER PEERS THROUGH THE SUN-FLECKED JUNGLE, TRYING TO LOCATE A TARGET, BUT THE JAPANESE, ONLY FIFTY YARDS AWAY, ARE QUIET.

LIBRARY OF CONGRESS, LC-USZ62-99192

**INFANTRYMEN WAIT AMONG MANGROVE ROOTS. ALTHOUGH THERE'S NO EVIDENCE OF IT,
ENEMY SOLDIERS WERE NEAR AND THEIR FIRE WOULD NOT HAVE BEEN UNEXPECTED.**

LIBRARY OF CONGRESS, LC-USZ62-50136

WHEN THE NAVY FINISHED SHELLING MAKIN AND THE PLANES STOPPED BOMBING, THE SOLDIERS STEPPED OFF THEIR LANDING CRAFT AND WADED ASHORE.

MARY ELLEN CESSNA

**STALKING SOME REMAINING JAPANESE SNIPERS, THREE INFANTRYMEN WALK PAST A BURNING
OIL DUMP, PART OF WHICH IS STILL ON FIRE AFTER NAVY SHELLING.**

MARY ELLEN CESSNA

A SOLDIER OF THE SHAMROCK BATTALION WAITS TO PUSH AHEAD.

(ABOVE) **EN ROUTE TO THE MARSHALLS, SERGEANT CHARLES BLAIR** (LEFT) **OF VERO BEACH, FLORIDA, SHARPENS THE EDGE OF HIS COMBAT KNIFE.**

LIBRARY OF CONGRESS, LC-USZ62-99195

(RIGHT) **THE WALLS OF THIS POWER PLANT ON ENNUBIRR ISLAND WERE TWO FEET THICK, BUT THAT WASN'T ENOUGH TO TAKE THE NAVY'S SHELLING.**

MARY ELLEN CESSNA

THE ORIGINAL CAPTION FOR THIS PHOTOGRAPH SAID: "WHILE SUPPLIES ARE
UNLOADED AT ENNUBIRR ISLAND, RESULT OF NAVY BOMBARDMENT CAN BE SEEN IN THE SKY."
THE LARGE EXPLOSION IN THE BACKGROUND, HOWEVER, COULD HAVE BEEN THE AFTERMATH
OF THE EXPLOSION OF A JAPANESE BLOCKHOUSE ON ROI THAT HAD BEEN FILLED WITH TORPE-
DOES AND AMMUNITION. THE EXPLOSION, WHICH KILLED APPROXIMATELY TWENTY MARINES
AND WOUNDED SEVERAL OTHERS, CAUSED ONE PILOT TO EXCLAIM:
"GREAT GOD ALMIGHTY! THE WHOLE DAMN ISLAND HAS BLOWN UP."

A BLASTED PILLBOX IS INSPECTED BY A MARINE WHOSE RIFLE IS READY SHOULD "DEAD" JAPANESE PROVE TO BE ALIVE.

**MOVING IN. WITH THE ENEMY ON THE BEACHES TAKEN CARE OF,
THESE MARINES MARCH OFF TO SEE WHAT'S AHEAD.**
LIBRARY OF CONGRESS

**MARINES STAND BY A WRECKED TANK AND TALK ABOUT THE BATTLE OF KWAJALEIN ATOLL
WHILE IN THE FOREGROUND REST A FEW OF THE THOUSANDS OF JAPANESE DEAD.**

LIBRARY OF CONGRESS, LC-USZ62-8712

(LEFT) **TWIN-MOUNTED DUAL-PURPOSE ANTI-AIRCRAFT GUNS WERE KNOCKED OUT BY SHELLS BEFORE THE FIRST AMERICAN TROOPS LANDED.**
LIBRARY OF CONGRESS

(ABOVE) **THIS WAS NO PLACE TO BE CHOOSY ABOUT THE BRAND OF YOUR BEER. THE STUFF HAPPENS TO BE JAPANESE.**
LIBRARY OF CONGRESS, LC-USZ62-97558

(LEFT) **THESE SOLDIERS ON THE BEACH OF ENIWETOK ISLAND IN THE MARSHALLS HAD JUST BEEN LANDED AND WERE AWAITING THE ORDER TO ATTACK WHEN THEY WERE PHOTOGRAPHED BY BUSHEMI. A LITTLE WHILE LATER THESE MEN MOVED AHEAD.**

LIBRARY OF CONGRESS, LC-USZ62-25604

(ABOVE) **WITH A MACHINE GUN ALREADY SET UP, SOLDIERS WIELD ENTRENCHING TOOLS TO SCOOP OUT A HOME.**

LIBRARY OF CONGRESS, LC-USZ62-8711

**WHEN WAR CAME TO ENIWETOK ISLAND THESE NATIVES HAD A RINGSIDE SEAT—SO NEAR THAT
SOME OF THEM HAVE TAKEN TO A FOXHOLE BECAUSE OF JAPANESE SNIPER FIRE.**

**THESE NATIVES OF ENIWETOK HAPPILY GREET AN AMERICAN GI WHO
RECENTLY LANDED ON THEIR ISLAND.**

LIBRARY OF CONGRESS

**THE LAST PICTURE BUSHEMI MADE: LIEUTENANT COLONEL MIZONY
HOLDS A CAPTURED JAPANESE FLAG.**
LIBRARY OF CONGRESS